Intentionally Left Blank

Intentionally Left Blank

Risky Business:

The Global Threat Network and the Politics of Contraband

THE COMBATING TERRORISM CENTER AT WEST POINT

Contents

AUTHOR ACKNOWLEDGMENTS

This project would not have come to fruition without the assistance of numerous individuals and organizations.

A special thank-you goes to World-Check at Thomson Reuters, and specifically John Solomon. John was a critical engine in building the relationship between World-Check and the Combating Terrorism Center that helped the project get off the ground. He also contributed to and provided valuable commentary throughout the project.

A number of individuals also helped improve this work substantially in different ways. Michael Kenney deserves special thanks for providing feedback on a prior draft and improving my understanding of crime and terror networks. Others such as John Archer, Robert Axelrod, Scott Carpenter, Brian Dodd, Karen Greenberg, Bruce Hoffman, Patrick Radden Keefe, Kristen Larsen, David Luna, Aleksander Matovski, John Picarelli, Mark Scraba, Troy Thomas, Janey Wright, Dominick Wright and Juan Zarate helped to inform the paper through fascinating and fruitful discussions on illicit networks over a long period of time. An excellent team of research assistants, including Paula Alfosnso, Carley St. Claire and Jay Chittooran, helped to make the project possible. There are countless others that could be listed.

The mentorship and intellectual guidance of GEN(R) John Abizaid, AMB Michael Sheehan and Vinnie Viola also merit special recognition for contributing insights and providing unwavering support. At the Combating Terrorism Center, Brian Dodwell, Daniel Milton and Bryan Price deserve thanks for feedback that helped improve the work immeasurably over repeated drafts. The rest of the CTC staff, and particularly Ryan Bell, Jon Brickey, Cindy Jebb, Arie Perliger, Don Rassler and Todd Schultz helped to shape the paper in invaluable ways.

There are undoubtedly errors in spite of the wonderful support that many have offered to this effort. Those errors are entirely my own.

Scott Helfstein
West Point, New York
May 2014

EXECUTIVE SUMMARY

This study looks at the interrelationship between illicit activity in the economic and political arenas. It offers a different perspective on the global illicit marketplace and the connectivity between crime and terror through examining the relationships of those who produce and profit from fear for financial or political purposes.

Looking across a range of illicit activities that include terrorism, the illegal narcotics trade, organized crime, human smuggling and political corruption, the network analysis includes 2,700 individuals linked by 15,000 relationships spanning 122 countries.

Conventional wisdom suggests that criminal-terrorist connectivity is a phenomenon found in failed and economically poor states. This argument relies on four assumptions: (1) poor economic conditions drive people into the illicit sectors; (2) criminal and terrorist actors are more likely to thrive in environments with weak governments and poverty; (3) because it is easy for terrorist and criminals to cooperate, they will; (4) governmental and illicit actors are adversaries. The results of this study suggest that there is good reason to question each of these assumptions and in turn to revisit the fundamental empirical data relating to and explanations of crime-terror connectivity.

This large-scale data analysis, in some ways the first of its kind, offers a number of conclusions:

- The criminals and terrorists are largely subsumed (98%) in a single network as opposed to operating in numerous smaller networks. Connectivity among actors within the illicit marketplace is relatively high. This should not be construed to say that the network is a cohesive organizational entity. The phenomenon observed and documented here is a self-organizing complex system built through social connections from the bottom up.
- By most measures of connectivity, terrorists are more central than almost all other types of criminals, second only to narcotics smugglers. The transnational nature of terrorist actors allows them to link disparate criminal groups.
- It does not appear that terrorists are shunned based on social norms or fear of inviting retribution from law enforcement, as many criminals seem willing to interact with terrorists. An empirical analysis of the network shows that 46% of

terrorists' connections are linked to actors involved in activities other than terrorism, while those involved in other illicit activities link to terrorists 35% of the time.

- Almost half of those in the network were not directly identified as being criminals or terrorists but were suspected for involvement in illicit activities. The prominence of these peripheral actors may reflect the importance of operating across the licit and the illicit spheres.

- The conventional wisdom that explains crime-terror connectivity as a product of failed or economically poor states is challenged here. Just because it is easy for criminals and terrorists to work together does not necessarily explain why they would. Three additional explanations are considered: the comparative advantage among criminals and terrorists in capable states, state sponsorship to augment state weaknesses and revolutionary state behavior.

- Generally speaking, connectivity between terrorists and criminals is highest in resource-rich countries that have little incentive to support substate actors (comparative advantage theory) and resource-poor countries that are incentivized to support criminal or terrorist groups (augment state capabilities theory).
  - o If the criminals are better than terrorists at producing resources and terrorists excel at producing political chaos, then members of the two groups have incentive to cooperate against capable and well-resourced law enforcement institutions (comparative advantage).
  - o There is an assumption that governments and illicit actors are adversaries. States that are prone to conflict frequently use substate proxies. State sponsorship of terrorism is a well-known phenomenon, but state sponsorship of crime in pursuit of national goals is also a problem that deserves to be studied (augment state capabilities).

A series of implications are derived from these empirical, justified conclusions:

- Despite the interest surrounding big data and data science, the results of data acquisition and utilization often falls short of their potential. The growing number of data sources and tools offers an opportunity to conduct unique analyses addressing difficult problems. Advancing this agenda will require

7

asking questions in unique ways and pursuing creative approaches to analyzing data.

- Strategies aimed at addressing crime-terror issues should reflect that such connectivity is a distributed issue and is not constrained to any one type of state. The data analysis here shows that 122 countries are connected by more than 1,000 transnational relationships.

- The emphasis placed on failed states by law enforcement and national security authorities is in part driven by a false assumption, namely, if the weak or nonexistent governments in failed states can be replaced with functional institutions, then the threat from criminal and terror groups will decline. This may be a red herring. Given that connectivity is a characteristic of wealthy and functioning states, then building a functioning government in a failed state does not necessarily reduce the threat from criminal and terror groups within that state.

- The challenge of combating crime-terror connectivity in many places lies at the intersection between licit and illicit activity. The illicit economy is estimated to be as large as 20%-30% of the global economy. That money is not put under mattresses or stashed in warehouses. And the line between the licit and illicit can be obscure in many contexts.

- Identifying financial irregularities is critical to tracking dirty money, questionable transactions and illicit actors. Many government agencies are not training their analysts in the intelligence or defense communities to think about the convergence of commerce, economics and threats. This skill gap represents a challenge confronting law enforcement and national security authorities.

- Authorizations will also play a critical role in attacking the global network of terror and crime. The Department of Defense assigns resources to such programs as counterterrorism, counternarcotics and counterproliferation discretely. The nature of crime-terror connectivity suggests that maintaining such rigid boundaries may not always be the most effective approach, and utilizing resources and techniques associated with counterterrorism in conjunction with counternarcotics may yield the best results.

- This project should not necessarily be interpreted as a call for new authorizations. Instead, actors across the interagency national security apparatus must understand the authorizations granted to partner organizations, in order to design more comprehensive strategies for tackling these interconnected challenges.

This study is one of the first comprehensive, open-source, data-driven assessments of the global transnational illicit network, leveraging a unique data source originally developed for financial compliance. The Combating Terrorism Center (CTC) worked with World-Check, which gathered the data that the CTC then structured and analyzed for this study. World-Check began the collection of its data in 2000, and such data continues to be compiled daily by a global team of 450 research specialists. The sources of this data include government and intergovernmental sanctions lists, legal filings, academic and policy institute research reports and global news and social media, as well as gray literature, including online journals and videos published by sanctioned groups.

INTRODUCTION

The next decade of counterterrorism operations will look drastically different from those of the previous ten years. The era of counterterrorism operations undertaken through large campaigns appears to be over, as the United States lacks the political will to enter into another large-scale conflict in the Middle East or Central Asia. Compared with counterterrorism operations in Afghanistan and Iraq, counterterrorism forces in the future will not benefit from the thick information networks that develop when conventional forces control a battle space. Instead, much of these operations will be conducted by small units or partner nations, with U.S. forces working at the behest of a local government in need of assistance. With the military aspect of counterterrorism in transition, two elements will prove critical to future success. The first is information on terrorist threats, and the second is upgrading the effective use of all the government's counterterrorism tools to include the insights of the law enforcement and financial communities.

Given this almost inevitable transition in counterterrorism strategy, building a good understanding of the global threat network, including the means by which it sustains itself, is more critical than ever. For some time, experts have debated the relationships between criminality and terrorism. Some argue that terrorists occasionally utilize crime or collaborate with criminals to generate resources for themselves but generally view criminal and terrorist networks as distinct entities. Others argue that the relationship between criminals and terrorists is relatively common, representing a new hybrid threat. Interestingly, both sides tend to use similar examples, such as al-Qa'ida in the Islamic Maghreb's use of kidnapping or Mexican drug-trafficking organizations' use of terror tactics such as beheadings. Anecdotes of that type have played a critical role in fostering the debate about the relationship between crime and terror, licit and illicit marketplaces, profit and principle.

This study offers a different perspective of the global illicit marketplace and the connectivity of crime and terrorism through examining the relationships of those who produce and profit from fear for financial or political purposes. Looking across a range of illicit activities that include terrorism, the illegal narcotics trade, organized crime, human smuggling and political corruption, this study presents a unique map of the illicit global marketplace. It also suggests that there is still a great deal more to learn.

The connectivity of terrorists and criminals is not a rare event but rather a ubiquitous feature of the global transnational illegal network. An analysis of this network shows that 98% of the 2,700 individuals included in this study are part of a single large network spanning 122 countries. These individuals are linked through a dense web of 15,000 relationships, and terrorists play a critical role in linking disparate criminal elements from around the world.

Given the assumption that terrorists and criminals increase their operational risks by working together, one may think that the fear of retribution from law enforcement would prevent such connectivity. This assumption does not seem to hold in the face of the data examined here. Explaining the connectivity between criminals and terrorists is a challenge, but such an explanation is critical to an intelligence-led counterterrorism effort. There are four different theories that explain the high levels of connectivity explored in this project: resource competition in failed or economically poor states, comparative advantage in capable states, state sponsorship to augment state weaknesses and revolutionary state behavior. The conventional argument, that connectivity is driven by poverty and state failure, is called the resource competition theory in this project.[1] This traditional story of the interaction among criminals and terrorists, however, misses certain vital elements such as the importance of negative political control and the state use of substate actors.

Failed states are often perceived as incubators for hybrid threats, and as such are often considered to be the perfect spaces for terrorists and criminals to collaborate away from law enforcement and counterterrorism forces. This argument is not supported in this

---

[1] Thomas, M. Sanderson, "Transnational Terror and Organized Crime: Blurring the Lines," *SAIS Review* 24, no. 1 (Winter-Spring 2004), 49–61; John Rollins and Liana Sun Wyler, "International Terrorism and Transnational Crime: Security Threats, U.S. Policy, and Considerations for Congress," Congressional Research Service, 18 March 2010; Hriar Cabayan, "Executive Summary," in *The "New" Face of Transnational Crime Organizations (TCOs): A Geopolitical Perspective and Implications for U.S. National Security*, eds. Ben Riley and Kathleen Kiernan (Strategic Multi-layer Assessment Occasional White Paper, May 2013), 5; Renee Novakoff et al., "Transnational Organized Crime: A USSOUTHCOM Perspective," in *The "New" Face of Transnational Crime Organizations (TCOs): A Geopolitical Perspective and Implications for U.S. National Security*, eds. Ben Riley and Kathleen Kiernan (Strategic Multi-layer Assessment Occasional White Paper, May 2013), 56.

analysis. Just because it is easy for terrorists and criminals to work together does not necessarily explain why they would. In fact, there is little incentive for these groups to collaborate in such environments. Terrorists operating in a failed state can easily commit crimes without the help of criminals, and criminals can easily scare parts of the population without the assistance of terrorists.

Crime-terror connectivity is common in two settings. The first is in rich countries, which tend to have capable law enforcement and counterterrorism forces. As opposed to the permissive environments in failed states, it is difficult for criminals and terrorists to operate in these places. At the same time, these countries' wealth and prestige make them attractive targets for both crime and terrorism. In these contexts there is comparative advantage in collaboration.

Terrorists have an interest in criminality, or in working with criminals, in order to secure the resources they need to sustain their campaigns. Criminals, for their part, as the traditional narrative goes, will work with terrorists provided that there is a potential for monetary profit. There is a critical missing element in this story, however. Criminals' interest in terrorist activity actually goes beyond profit, since criminals also desire a sanctuary or the political space from which to operate with less pressure from the government or from law enforcement agencies.[2] They do not wish to govern the space (what might be thought of as taking positive political control), but they do wish to deny others the ability to do so (what might be called negative political control). Although criminals excel at exploiting markets to produce profits, terrorists excel at challenging the government and making it more difficult to for the government to assert political control.

The second setting in which high levels of criminal and terrorist connectivity are common is in poor countries that tend to engage in many international disputes. Sates have frequently used proxies and substate forces to achieve political aims that may not

_____

[2] Patrick Radden Keefe, "The Geography of Badness: Mapping the Hubs of the Illicit Global Economy," in *Convergence*, eds. Michael Miklaucic and Jacqueline Brewer (Washington, DC: National Defense University Press, 2013), available at www.ndufoundation.org/file/pdf-test/Convergence.pdf.

have been legitimate for the state itself to pursue.[3] A modern incarnation of this is seen in relationships such as Pakistan's support for Lashkar-e-Taybha (LeT) and Iran's sponsorship of Hezbollah.[4] While certain states support militant groups to achieve their political ends, criminal enterprises are generally assumed to operate at odds with a government rather than at its bidding. This obscures the role that states may play in maintaining a criminal enterprise to achieve certain economic or political ends.

For example, Pakistan's Inter-Service Intelligence (ISI) has worked with Dawood Ibrahim's criminal enterprise known as D-Company, Slobodan Milosevic cultivated an organized crime syndicate to subvert oil sanctions and many of Russia's primary political clans each have criminal wings with ties to the security service.[5] The same security and intelligence agencies that build, sustain and liaise with substate terrorist groups for political purposes often have parallel relationships with criminal groups. Since these groups have similar origins and handlers in the security and intelligence worlds, these deep connections are perhaps not surprising.

The empirical findings here suggest a fundamental need to revisit our assumptions about the structure of the global threat network; the social infrastructure that links terrorists and criminals; the role of failed states; the tools that will be most effective in countering a thick web of global threats, including terrorism; and the role of data in understanding how best to counter threats.

This study paints an unconventional picture of the global threat network, because of the way it uses data. Despite the interest surrounding big data and data science in the public and private sectors, the results of data acquisition and utilization often fall short of their potential. Often, vast amounts of open-source data are ignored, data that are

---

[3] Grant Wardlaw, "Terror as an instrument of foreign policy," *Journal of Strategic Studies* 10, no. 4 (1987), 237–259.

[4] Daniel Byman, *Deadly Connections: States that Sponsor Terrorism* (Cambridge: Cambridge University Press, 2005).

5 For a discussion of D-Company, see Ryan Clarke and Stuart Lee, "The PIRA, D-Company, and the Crime-Terror Nexus," *Terrorism and Political Violence* 20, no. 3 (October 2008), 376–395; for a discussion of Yugoslavia, see Peter Andreas, "Criminalizing Consequences of Sanctions: Embargo Busting and Its Legacy," *International Studies Quarterly* 49, no. 2 (2005), 335–360; for a discussion of Russia, see Mark Galeotti, *Russian and Post-Soviet Organized Crime* (London: Ashgate, 2002).

leveraged are rarely structured in ways amenable to methodologically sound analysis and the resulting outputs are usually in the form of basic anecdotes or visuals. As a result, there remains a shortage of rigorous research on or assessment of issues that are increasingly accessible. The growing number of data sources, and the evolving open-source space, offer an opportunity to conduct unique analyses addressing difficult problems. Advancing this agenda will require asking questions in unique ways and pursuing creative approaches to analyzing data.

The next section of this paper takes a closer look at the definitions of crime and terrorism, as well as at the main debates about the so-called nexus at which they interact. This is followed by a brief discussion about the data, providing a snapshot of World-Check's database and an overview of the coding methodology. The report then focuses on the "pseudoexperiment" used to construct the network map that drives the subsequent analyses. After walking through the mapping process, the next section explores the empirical characteristics of the 2,700-person dark network, including assessments of the network structure, the relative connectivity of criminals and terrorists and the geographical distribution of transnational illicit relationships. This is followed by a deep dive into the four competing theories that aim to explain crime-terror connectivity. The final empirical section of the paper tests these four competing arguments and suggests that two have strong support while two do not. The paper then concludes by reviewing the major conclusions and considering their potential policy implications.

with John Solomon

Convergence among criminal and terrorist elements remains a contested subject among the relatively limited set of experts and policy makers who focus on the issue.[6] Some have argued that the process of convergence, usually defined as the increased interaction among criminals and terrorists, has continued apace, and that this growing interconnected network presents a unique problem that threatens national security.[7] Others have argued that the convergence thesis is overblown and that although the temporary marriage of convenience that often arises from such increased interaction is disconcerting, it is far from a significant national security threat.[8] It is hard to dispute the growing complexity that is resulting from Internet-driven technologies and a greater international interconnectedness through ideological affinity or shared economic interest across an array of illicit activities.

Crime and Terrorism

Before focusing on convergence, the dominant arguments surrounding it and the counterpoints to those arguments, it is important to define the terms "crime" and "terrorism." That said, this report will make some simplifications, as there are many definitions of "terrorism" identified by earlier research.[9] Similarly, "crime" is often defined differently across jurisdictions.

---

[6] For a summary of this debate, see John T. Picarelli, "A Brief Discussion of the Nature and Convergence of Transnational Organized Crime and Terrorism," paper prepared for the Trans-Atlantic Dialogue on Combating Crime-Terror Pipelines, 25–26 June 2012; John T. Picarelli, "Osama bin Corleone? Vito the Jackal? Framing Threat Convergence Through an Examination of Transnational Organized Crime and International Terrorism," *Terrorism and Political Violence* 24, no. 2 (2012).

[7] Thomas M. Sanderson, "Transnational Terror and Organized Crime: Blurring the Lines," *SAIS Review* 24, no. 1 (Winter/Spring 2004), 49–61; Bob Killebrew and Jennifer Bernal, *Crime Wars: Gangs, Cartels and U.S. National Security* (Washington, DC: Center for New American Studies, 2010).

[8] Christopher Dishman, "Terrorism, Crime and Transformation," *Studies in Conflict and Terrorism* 24, no. 1 (2001), 43–58.

[9] A. Peter Schmid and Albert Jongman, *Political Terrorism* (Amsterdam: North Holland Publishing, 1988), 1–38.

While numerous articles have been composed with the sole purpose of defining terrorism, and the UN still operates without a common definition of it, there are several common features across definitions. For the purposes of this report, "terrorism" here is not a normative label, meaning that no distinction is made between those who use terrorist tactics for ostensibly "good" reasons and those whose motives are "bad." Terrorism, for our purposes, occurs when someone uses a terrorist tactic, meaning when he or she employs violence or the threat of violence against civilians with the purpose of achieving a psychological effect to achieve a political goal.[10] This violence is often discriminate and targeted, but the victims of the violence are not necessarily the targets of the attack. In that sense, terrorism is about communication, and the violence itself is often symbolic, with ramifications beyond the immediate act.[11] The political ends for which terrorism is employed may be motivated by ideological, political or religious convictions. Further, terrorism today is often used in the context of substate actors. That is not to say that states have not, or do not, commit terrorist acts. Rather, terrorism in this paper is limited to substate actors.

Crime is generally defined as an unlawful act for which the perpetrator can be punished by a government. Within the broad classification of crime, organized groups often represent a unique challenge to law enforcement agencies. Like the definition of terrorism, there is no universal definition of organized crime. The UN Convention Against Organized Transnational Crime provides a fairly comprehensive definition of organized crime, involving a structured group of at least three individuals formed with the intent of committing one or more serious crimes to obtain material benefit.[12] While this definition does not cover all possible types of crime (for example, petty larceny

---

[10] Bruce Hoffman, *Inside Terrorism* (New York: Columbia University Press, 2006); Boaz Ganor, "Defining Terrorism: Is One Man's Terrorist Another Man's Freedom Fighter?," *Police Practice and Research: An International Journal* 3, no. 4 (2002), 287–304.

[11] Andrew Kydd and Barbara Walter, "The Strategies of Terrorism," *International Security* 31, no. 1 (2006), 49–80.

[12] According to the UN convention, organized crime involves "a structured group that is not randomly formed for the immediate commission of an offense of three or more persons, existing for a period of time and acting in concert with the aim of committing one or more serious crimes or offenses punishable by a deprivation of liberty of at least four years established in accordance with this convention in order to obtain, directly or indirectly, a financial or other material benefit."

carried out by a single individual), it covers higher-value illicit economic activities including trafficking in narcotics, arms and people. The 179 UN member states that have ratified the UNCAC convention indicate a generally accepted international consensus in regard to this definition. In addition, many scholarly and policy-related works addressing crime and terrorism use this definition.[13]

It is important to remember that terrorist acts are invariably a form of serious crime in the sense that such acts often unlawfully target civilians, and their perpetrators seek to achieve something of benefit by means of such acts. By contrast, crime is not necessarily and most often not an act of terrorism. Extending that logic, all terrorist are criminals, but most criminals or criminal groups do not use terrorist tactics and should not be labeled as terrorists.

Perhaps the most common distinction seen by academics and operational elements drawn between terrorists and other criminals centers on the motives of the respective individuals or groups.[14] Traditional criminals violate the law with the purpose of profit maximization. They may pursue power, but economic motives reign supreme. Terrorists act for political or ideological purposes, often with the intent of exerting political power. Terrorist tactics are often used as an instrument to alter, or at least to attempt to alter, a government's decision-making calculus.

Despite such efforts to draw clear distinctions between crime and terrorism, certain aspects of each blur the lines between these two concepts. First, both criminal and terrorist groups operate clandestinely, as participants in the illicit marketplace. The clandestine nature of their operations means that analysts and policy makers can easily observe only a portion of such a group's activities. Second, each of these two groups has a tendency to pursue similar activities. For example, criminal groups often target public officials, law enforcement officials or civilians who threaten to obstruct their profit realization. This looks like terrorism, but with a different motive. Likewise, terrorist

---

[13] John R. Wagley, "Transnational Organized Crime: Principal Threats and U.S. Responses," in *CRS Report for Congress* (Washington: Congressional Research Service, 2006).

[14] Louise I. Shelley and John T. Picarelli, "Methods Not Motives: Implications of the Convergence of International Organized Crime and Terrorism," *Police Practice and Research: An International Journal* 3, no. 4 (2002), 305–318.

groups often pursue criminal activities such as narcotics trafficking or extortion to fund their operations. At this blurry intersection, analysts have developed a concept called crime-terror convergence.

Convergence

Astute analysts who have unpacked the idea of convergence suggest that one must look across different facets of it. The most common distinction is between convergence in activity and convergence in organizations.[15] Activity convergence occurs when terrorists employ criminal activities or criminals use terrorist tactics in pursuit of their respective political and economic ends. Organizational convergence occurs when terrorist groups and criminal enterprises work together.

The literature often refers to activity convergence as activity appropriation, since the group employing such a convergence ostensibly borrows the operational profile of the other.[16] More often than not, activity appropriation occurs when terrorist groups rely on crime to fund their operations and organizations. The Basque separatist group Euskadi ta Askatasuna (ETA) and the Sri Lankan separatist organization Liberation Tigers of Tamil Eelam (LTTE) both used extortion to generate a "revolutionary tax" from local populations and businesses in the late 20th century.[17] More recently, the Islamic State of Iraq, al-Qa'ida's umbrella network in Iraq, raised substantial funds from the underground trafficking of stolen Islamic antiquities during the Iraq War.[18] Al-Qa'ida in the Islamic Maghreb's (AQIM) success in kidnapping for ransom has essentially

---

[15] Philip Williams, "Terrorism and Organized Crime: Convergence, Nexus or Transformation?" in *Report on Terrorism*, ed. G. Jervas (Stockholm: Swedish Defence Research Establishment, 1998), 69–92; Michael Kenney, *From Pablo to Osama: Trafficking and Terrorist Networks, Government Bureaucracies, and Competitive Adaptation* (University Park, PA: Pennsylvania State University Press, 2007); and P. Lowe, "Counterfeiting: Links to Organised Crime and Terrorist Funding." *Journal of Financial Crime* 13, no. 2 (2006), 255–257.

[16] Shelley and Picarelli, 2002.

[17] Shawn Teresa Flanigan, "Nonprofit Service Provision by Insurgent Organizations: The Cases of Hizballah and the Tamil Tigers," *Studies in Conflict and Terrorism* 31, no. 6 (2008), 499–519.

[18] Elena Becatoros, "Smuggled Antiquities Funding Iraq Extremists, U.S. Says," *National Geographic News*, 19 March 2008, available at http://news.nationalgeographic.com/news/2008/03/080319-AP-iraq-insurg.html .

underwritten the coup and civil war in Mali.[19] Other well-documented examples include the Revolutionary Armed Forces of Colombia (FARC) and the Abu Sayyaf group in the Philippines, both of which came to rely on narcotics and extortion-related revenue to fund their operations.

While many people generally overlook criminals' use of terrorist tactics, criminal organizations often use terrorism as a tool to manipulate politicians, law enforcement and the public.[20] Organized crime groups have often resorted to assassinations to avoid government intervention and to frighten a population. The Bulgarian mob, for example, has been involved in a number of assassinations since the mid-1990s, including those of a former prime minister and a mayor.[21] The Mexican drug organizations have escalated both their violence and their activity appropriation in recent years with the use of beheadings and vehicle-borne improvised explosive devices (VBIEDs).[22] Video documentation of their attacks, often targeting civilians in marketplaces and the like, are regularly shared publicly via YouTube, suggesting an intent to communicate symbolically through terrorist violence. The criminal and narcotrafficking gang MS-13 was sanctioned by the U.S. Department of the Treasury after escalating terrorist violence in El Salvador.[23]

Organizational convergence differs from activity appropriation in that it involves two groups working together rather than the unilateral appropriation of one group's set of tactics by the other. Unlike activity appropriation, which may be short-lived, convergence among groups is generally perceived as a long-term activity that goes beyond a single illegal narcotics transaction or arms deal. Organizational convergence

---

[19] Hanna Rogan, "Al-Qaida in the Islamic Maghreb Strikes Again," *Perspectives on Terrorism* 2, no. 8 (2008). http://terrorismanalysts.com/pt/index.php/pot/article/view/46/html.

[20] Tamara Makarenko, "The Crime-Terror Continuum: Tracing the Interplay between Transnational Organised Crime and Terrorism," *Global Crime* 6, no. 1 (2004), 129–145.

[21] Misha Glenny, *McMafia: A Journey Through the Global Criminal Underworld* (New York: Random House, 2008).

[22] William Booth, "Ciudad Juarez car bomb shows new sophistication in Mexican drug cartels' tactics," *Washington Post*, 22 July 2010, available at www.washingtonpost.com/wp-dyn/content/article/2010/07/21/AR2010072106200.html.

[23] Department of the Treasury, "Treasury Sanctions Latin American Criminal Organization," 11 October 2012, available at www.treasury.gov/press-center/press-releases/Pages/tg1733.aspx.

such as the Haqqani network's relationship with al-Qa'ida and D-Company's relationship with Lashkar-e-Taybha occurs with some frequency, and the duration can vary widely.[24] Vahid Brown and Don Rassler have used primary source material to show that the Haqqani relationship with al-Qa'ida goes back two decades. There are a number of documented cases of organizational convergence in the last twenty years. The former Irish Republican Army (IRA) and the Ulster Defense Association (UDA) provided protection for smuggling and prostitution enterprises run by Italians, Serbians and Chinese Triads in Northern Ireland.[25] In exchange, these criminal organizations supplied opportunities in illicit markets such as that of counterfeit luxury goods. The IRA and UDA were thought at one time to control the vast majority of the local trade in such items. In Latin America, terrorist groups like the Shining Path and the Paraguayan People's Army (EPP) worked with narcotics traffickers. Overall, organizational convergence takes different forms. Common areas of convergence include the arms business, the illegal narcotics trade, protection for smuggling, and extortion, and may also include activities such as assassinations and bomb-making.

The paradigm that distinguishes between activity and organizational convergence is helpful, but it can also be misleading as groups evolve, the operating landscape shifts, groups' membership change or the role of ideology changes. Appending the label "criminal" or "terrorist" on a particular organization that may or may not always be consistent with its raison d'être, objectives and motivations could create problems for countering such groups in the future. This concern lies at the center of an alternative approach in the convergence literature referred to as "motives not means."[26] Rather than focus on the activities that an organization undertakes, this approach suggests that it is more important to look at the underlying motivations of both organizations and individuals. The focus on motivations can help to clarify the root causes of behavior,

---

[24] On the Haqqanis and al-Qa'ida, see Vahid Brown and Don Rassler, *Fountainhead of Jihad: The Haqqani Nexus, 1973–2012* (New York: Columbia University Press, 2012); on D-Company and LeT, see Rollins and Wyler, 2010.

[25] David Lister and Sean O'Neill, "IRA plc turns from terror into biggest crime gang in Europe," *The Times*, 25 February 2005, available at www.thetimes.co.uk/tto/news/uk/article1932704.ece; R. T. Naylor, *Wages of Crime: Black Markets, Illegal Finance, and the Underworld Economy* (New York: Columbia University Press, 2004).

[26] Shelley and Picarelli, 2002.

and, for example, help to identify a group largely engaged in criminal activity as a terrorist group if its ultimate ends are political in nature.

The "motives not means" approach is powerful in the sense that it serves as a reminder to avoid attribution error and assess what groups aim to accomplish. That said, one of the constraints to validating this paradigm is that motivations or intent are often masked, or at the very least are opaque. Analysts and law enforcement officials can observe a robbery or a bombing, but they cannot see inside the culprit's head to divine his or her underlying motivations. This is often more challenging at the individual level, but easier to discern when it comes to groups. Groups, terrorist and criminal, often communicate with some frequency, making demands or propaganda statements. Memoirs can also be helpful in this regard. That said, when the "motives not means" approach is applied at the group level, which is where it is commonly used, an extra complication arises from the divergent priorities that may be present among a group's members.[27] Some members of a group may be more motivated by ideological and political ends, while others may be more motivated by the economic benefits of membership. This is the classic problem that Robert Jervis and Graham Allison each addressed in different ways when challenging the paradigm of the monolithic Soviet Union during the Cold War.[28] Individual perspectives, according to both analysts, varied greatly and were driven by divergent interests and personal biases.

Another problem that arises within the convergence and motives paradigms is that both tend to emphasize groups. Studies of organizational convergence or motives frequently find it challenging to define the limits of the groups under study and to identify where

---

[27] On divergence in of interests, see Scott Helfstein, "Governance of Terror: New Institutionalism and the Evolution of Terrorist Organizations," *Public Administration Review* 69 (2009), 727–739; Jacob N. Shapiro and David Siegel "Moral Hazard, Discipline, and the Management of Terrorist Organizations," *World Politics* 64 (2012), 39–78.

[28] Graham Allison and Philip Zelikow, *Essence of Decision: Explaining the Cuban Missile Crisis* (New York, NY: Longman, 1971; 2nd ed., 1999); Robert Jervis, *Perception and Misperception in International Politics* (Princeton, NJ: Princeton University Press, 1976).

one group ends and another begins.[29] For example, an individual like Illyas Kashmiri reportedly has had relationships with Harkat-ul-Jihad al-Islami (Huji), LeT, al-Qa'ida and D-Company.[30] Affixing him to any one of those entities risks underestimating convergence, but considering him as a part of all those entities complicates topology. Simplifying associations or drawing firm boundaries around groups allows one to examine convergence at the cost of addressing some of the challenges of definition tied to activity appropriation. For example, it is difficult to determine whether beheadings conducted by Mexican drug organizations are terrorist or criminal actions.

The convergence debate has helped analysts better understand and classify groups' behavior, but it is unclear whether the act of crime-terror convergence itself represents a serious threat to national security. One side suggests that crime is an endemic part of the global economic system, and while it helps to foster terrorism, it is not in and of itself a threat to national security.[31] Using the same series of convergence paradigms, others suggest that the intersection of crime and terrorism increases the likelihood of facing either ideological criminals or resource-supercharged terrorists with limited or no restraints on violence.[32] Further national security concerns arise since the transnational nature of these threats limits any single country's ability to mount a meaningful response to this global problem.

There are a few common assumptions and conclusions in the convergence debate, and these provide the departure points for this inquiry. The first is that a world of difference exists between the motives of terrorists and criminals.[33] This seems to be a common

---

[29] For a discussion on the breakdown of hierarchies and how that complicates understanding of illicit networks, see Chris Dishman, "The Leaderless Nexus: When Crime and Terror Converge," *Studies in Conflict and Terrorism* 28, no. 3 (2004), 237–252.

[30] C. Christine Fair, "Lashkar-e-Tayiba and the Pakistani State," *Survival: Global Politics and Strategy* 53, no. 4 (2011), 29–52.

[31] Todd Sandler, "On the Relationship Between Democracy and Terrorism," *Terrorism and Political Violence* 7, no, 4 (1995), 1–9.

[32] S. Chakravarty, "The dons of terror: Aftab Ansari and Omar Sheikh," *India Today*, 25 February 2002; Svante E. Cornell, "Narcotics and Armed Conflict: Interaction and Implications," *Studies in Conflict and Terrorism* 30, no. 3 (2007), 207–227.

[33] R. Naylor, *Wages of Crime: Black Markets, Illegal Finance and the Underworld Economy* (Ithaca, NY: Cornell University Press, 2002).

assumption even among those who see convergence as a threat. Second, there is also a tendency, particularly present among those who do not see convergence as a threat, to discount long-lasting convergence.[34] The underlying logic beneath this tendency states that criminals want little to do with terrorism, given risks such as the possibility of facing government antiterrorism capabilities or the stigma associated with such associations. This then provides the avenue for causal arguments about convergence. Given this fear, criminals should be more apt to work with terrorists in ungoverned spaces where there is little fear from law enforcement.[35] One could further hypothesize that both terrorists and criminals share a desire for operating in ungoverned spaces (but in fact there is mixed evidence to support this argument). This causal argument about convergence is sometimes carried one step further to suggest that illicit markets are more likely to prosper in underdeveloped countries, whereas globalization and economic development serve as a check on illicit activity.[36] There are good reasons to question many of these causal arguments, particularly given the anecdotal nature of the evidence used to evaluate them.

The activity, organizational and motivational approaches to understanding convergence have led to some divergent hypotheses about illicit markets, crime-terror behavior and the threat to national security. A different analytical approach may help to cast the illicit marketplace, as well as the overlap of criminals and terrorists, in a new light. To achieve this purpose, this project adopts a slightly different method of assessing convergence than those discussed previously. Rather than focus on activities and organizations, though these factors are considered, this project focuses on how the network is built, by mapping individuals and their relationships to others. The research presented here on the transnational illicit marketplace, in some ways the first of its kind, examines convergence while accounting for motives and trying to avoid some of the

---

[34] Dishman, 2001; Naylor, 2002.

[35] John T. Picarelli, "The Turbulent Nexus Of Transnational Organised Crime And Terrorism: A Theory of Malevolent International Relations," *Global Crime* 7, no. 1 (2006), 1–24.; Rollins and Wyler, 2010; Cabayan, 2013.

[36] Peter Andreas, "Illicit international political economy: the clandestine side of globalization," *Review of International Political Economy* 11, no. 3 (August 2004), 641–652; Ching-Chi Hsieh and M. D. Pugh, "Poverty, Income Inequality, and Violent Crime: A Meta-Analysis of Recent Aggregate Data Studies," *Criminal Justice Review* 18, no. 2 (Autumn 1993), 182–202.

traditional pitfalls that have limited empirical study of it. It is important to recognize that there are limits to this exercise, which are discussed at greater length below, but by focusing on individuals as the base unit, this study presents an opportunity to develop a new picture of the global interconnectivity between terrorists and criminals.

Neither school of thought in the convergence debate has conclusively argued its side, but both perspectives have called for more data-driven empirical analysis to move the discussion forward. In response to this need, and in order to assess the state of convergence, the research team applied advanced analytics to the unique data in World-Check.

ACCESSING AND CODING DATA ON ILLICIT ACTIVITY

with John Solomon

Many studies of crime-terror convergence have relied on case studies that reflect aspects of either organizational ties or operational similarities between criminals and terrorists. Some of this literature has pushed beyond case studies to map specific networks and then used a comparative analysis to explain how convergence differs across contexts—for example, how Mexican drug organizations' use of terror tactics to frighten a population is different from D-Company's facilitation of terrorism in South Asia.[37] Thus far, there are few studies that rely on quantitative assessments, in part because of a lack of available data. Mining local media sources and court documents for research often limits the scope of a project, based on the geographic access or the language skills of the researchers.

This study is one of the first comprehensive, open-source, data-driven assessments of the global transnational illicit network, leveraging a unique data source originally developed for financial institutions to mitigate regulatory and reputation risks. The Combating Terrorism Center (CTC) worked with World-Check, a Thomson Reuters business, which gathered the data that the CTC then structured and used for this research study. Following the September 11 attacks, a series of federal regulations imposed stricter requirements on financial institutions. National and international regulatory and standards-setting organizations implemented rules and guidelines requiring financial institutions and other businesses to conduct due diligence on their clients' relationships in order to help prevent terrorist financing and other financial crimes. One of the traditional pillars of the anti–money laundering platform known as Know Your Customer (KYC), which requires due diligence on heightened-risk individuals and organizations as outlined by the Financial Action Task Force's recommendations, is the de facto international standard for countering financial crime and the illicit use of the global financial system. As a result, companies developed proprietary databases of individuals and organizations meeting heightened-risk categories (for example, politically exposed persons, such as an individual holding

---

[37] Clarke and Lee, 2008; Rollins and Wyler, 2010.

national public office, suspicious and blacklisted individuals as well as those falling on government blacklists such as the U.S. Treasury's Office of Foreign Asset Control list or the UN al-Qa'ida Sanctions List.

World-Check is the largest, most comprehensive commercially available database of heightened-risk people and organizations from around the world. The database includes not only politically exposed persons and government sanctioned entities, but also related illicit networks engaged in organized crime and terrorism. More than 6,000 international banks, businesses and nonprofits, as well as hundreds of law enforcement, intelligence and regulatory bodies, rely on World-Check to identify or mitigate regulatory and reputation risk.

World-Check began the collection of its data in 2000 and such data continues to be compiled daily by a global team of 450 research specialists. The database today contains more than 2 million unique profiles of individuals and organizations. Subject-matter specialists with regional and linguistic expertise process and structure the data for use in low-latency information processing environments for businesses and government agencies. The data are drawn from online open sources in more than sixty-two languages, including Arabic, Mandarin and Russian. The sources of this data include government and intergovernmental sanctions lists, legal filings, academic and policy institute research reports and global news and social media, as well as gray literature, including online journals and videos published by sanctioned groups. The legal filings come from over eighty countries and the sanctions list includes all the major entities, including the U.S., Eurozone, Interpol and the UN. Court filings are not limited to convictions, but include indictments as well, providing a rich data source. Since many of the individuals at the center of this study represent the most significant criminal and terrorist threats, both past and present, much of the data on these people is drawn from court filings and sanction lists. As one moves from kingpins to those on the periphery of the illicit network, the data are increasingly drawn from open-source reporting.

The structured biographical intelligence profiles used in the World-Check database follow a format well known in the intelligence and law enforcement communities. This format includes the known name, alias, locations, known associates, national identity number, date of birth, risk-relevant reporting and judicial data of an individual. These records are also categorized by crime and terrorism identifier as driven by official government designations and organizational affiliations. These categories include: Terrorism; Crime–Narcotics; Crime–Organized; Crime–Financial; Crime–War; Crime–Other; and individuals of heightened risk as it relates to financial crime (which is referred to hereafter as Suspicious Individual).[38]

An individual's profile is included in the database when an official designation is made placing him or her in one of the categories described above, when a court proceeding against an individual for a crime in one of the above categories is undertaken, or when sufficient evidence exists to warrant further due diligence be undertaken on an individual's financial accounts. Each individual in the database has received a single designation for his or her activity, a designation that is most frequently derived from legal designations and filings. For example, individuals designated as terrorists by the United States, the European Union, or the United Nations are coded as such in the activity data field. Other individuals under the "terrorism" risk category may not necessarily have been explicitly designated as such, but may have been convicted of a terrorist offense, or, in some cases, have self-identified as a member of a designed network via a documented source. Similarly, those designated for transnational criminal activity or targeted in court proceedings as participants in either the illegal narcotics trade or organized crime are coded to reflect their activities as such.[39]

Government designations tend to be comprehensive when targeting a specific group in the sense that they are applied both to the members of a group and to those who provide any form of material support to the group. Therefore, for categorization

---

[38] Many of the individuals in this study are directly linked to actors involved in an array of criminal activities and thus constitute suspicious individuals. The World-Check database, because of financial compliance regulations, maintains a significant list of politically exposed persons (often referred as PEPs) who might have no involvement in criminal activities, but for whom financial institutions are supposed to be extra careful or vigilant.

[39] It is important to note that affixing any single label on an individual, particularly those individuals involved in illicit activity, is difficult. Prior efforts to code roles within terrorist organizations have been similarly constrained. Individuals may be committed to a terrorist group and commit a criminal act like theft, and the opposite may also be true. Use of government designations and criminal charges provided one way for World-Check to code illicit activity. The categorization process recognizes these challenges and tries to incorporate motivation where appropriate, and distinctions are opaque. There are limitations to any categorization, but it offers a way of systemically studying a complex issue.

purposes, the government designation (for example, Special Designated Global Terrorist) generally drives the categorization of an affiliated individual in the World-Check database, irrespective of the individual's particular activity. A member of a designated organized crime group who individually was reported to have used terrorist tactics would in general retain the category of the organizational parent, in this case, organized crime, rather than terrorism. A known al-Qa'ida member who was identified to have been involved in the illegal narcotics trade would still remain in the terrorism category in the World-Check database.

One other advantage in using World-Check is that the database is a "living" resource in a sense. Unlike many academic databases that are constructed and put online for historical use, World-Check must be vigilant in keeping the database updated to meet its customers' needs. This has two advantages: First, as new individuals involved in illicit activity come to light, World-Check opens up new files and begins cataloging information. Second, and equally as important, individuals inaccurately designated or indicted are removed from the database. This helps prevent false positives. Since the data here were taken at a snapshot in time, there may be some false positives, but the nature of the database helps minimize this risk.

The coding of illicit activity in the World-Check database served as a method of generating a double-blind procedure for the pseudoexperiment. Those involved in the methods and analytics portion of the research did not code the individuals in the database and simply used the existing designations upon the conclusion of the network mapping. That is to say, no subjective judgment was made on the activities of the individuals in the sample by the CTC research team that may have affected the study's results. The research team specifically focused on interpersonal connections, activities and geographic areas of operation. These data were then structured to conduct network and econometric analysis.

METHOD FOR MAPPING THE NETWORK

The project started with a simple set of questions: How do terrorists and transnational criminals intersect? What are the patterns of connectivity, and what are the potential drivers of this connectivity? The researchers of this study designed and conducted a pseudoexperiment to answer these questions. Since the emphasis of this study is the convergence of criminal and terrorist connections, and specifically the prominence of terrorists' ties to criminal networks, the first step involved developing a list of major transnational smugglers.[40] This initial list targeted individuals operating in the areas of illegal narcotics, arms and people smuggling. This exercise leveraged a wide range of sources, including Drug Enforcement Administration (DEA) briefs, media accounts and reports produced by nongovernmental organizations focused on major smugglers, or kingpin-type characters, operating over the past decade.[41] The list included actors from Latin and South America, the United States, Europe and Asia. The majority of the individuals on this list of major transnational smugglers were involved in the illegal narcotics trade, followed by a smaller number of those involved in the illegal arms trade, and finally those involved in trafficking humans. This is not intended to suggest that fewer people worldwide are involved in the illegal trade of arms or humans than those involved in the illegal drug trade, but rather that the majority of transnational characters prone to attracting significant attention among law enforcement agencies and open-source reports are those who are linked to narcotics. A sample of these individuals can be found in Appendix A.

---

[40] This list was assembled in consultation with law enforcement agencies such as the Drug Enforcement Administration, Immigration and Customs Enforcement and Customs Border Protection as well as open-source assessments of major criminal activity.

[41] By focusing on the kingpins—individuals who have amassed significant wealth and operate across many jurisdictions—this study emphasizes those who are relatively connected. A random sample of small-time criminals might not reveal the same patterns in connectivity, or it might require going deeper into a social network or undertaking a snowball sampling process to identify similar patterns.

Many studies of social networks rely on a method commonly referred to as a snowball sample.[42] In traditional snowball experiments, respondents are asked who they know, which provides the raw data for an "ego network" that puts a single person at its middle. The people around the central node or person ("Node-0") are referred to as the first degree connections. Experiments then frequently build on that baseline by asking each of the first degree connections who they know. Like a snowball, the further one goes from the first individual at the center of the ego network, the larger the network graph usually becomes. While snowball method does not produce a random and representative sample that serves as a cornerstone of experimental methodology, it does provide an effective approach to building a network map.

Figure 1: Degrees in Social Network Analysis

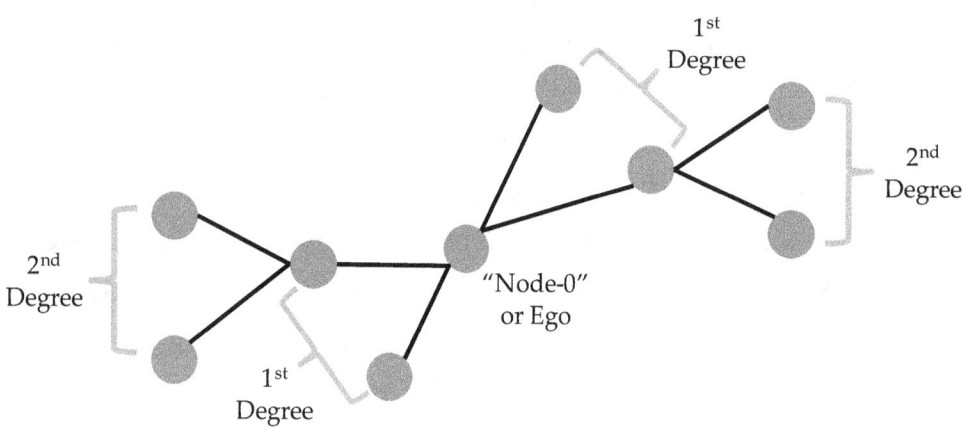

The empirical assessment undertaken here leveraged a modified approach to a snowball sample that attempts to mitigate some of the problems with conventional snowball sampling. Instead of selecting one individual to serve as Node-0 in the network graph, one might select a number of different individuals to serve as starting points for the acquisition of data. By selecting different people in different locations at the outset of mapping connections, such an approach minimizes the likelihood of simply winding up with a single connected network. In traditional snowball samples, by definition, one can only enter the network if he or she is connected to Node-0 by

[42] Noel M. Tichy, Michael L. Tushman and Charles Fombrun, "Social Network Analysis for Organizations," *The Academy of Management Review* 4, no. 4 (1979), 507–519; Gwen Moore, "The Structure of a National Elite Network," *American Sociological Review* 44, no. 5 (October 1979), 673–692

some acquaintance or an acquaintance of an acquaintance. This is displayed in Figure 1, where the first degree is shown to connect directly to Node-0, and the second degree is shown to be one step removed. If ten different people are selected in ten different countries, there should be a lower likelihood that their ego-networks intersect than if they were selected from the same country or region. One is more likely to end up with a series of parallel networks rather than one large network.

Table 1: Kingpin Characteristics for Snowball Samples

Region	% of Individuals	Arms	Humans	Narcotics
Africa	5%	3%	0%	2%
Asia	24%	9%	7%	9%
Europe	14%	12%	2%	0%
North America/Carribean	40%	5%	5%	29%
South America	17%	5%	2%	10%
Total	100%	34%	16%	50%

Table 1 shows the type of illicit activity in which the key traffickers were involved, according to their geographic region. Forty individuals seemed to offer a reasonable spread of activities and geography. The distribution reflected some interesting patterns. Different types of illicit activity are clustered in specific regions; the particular type of activity is often driven by the availability of illicit goods or jurisdictional operational advantages. There were no major human traffickers identified on the list from Africa and no major narcotics kingpins based in Europe. This does not mean that major criminal figures are absent in these areas, but only that the list devised here did not include them.[43] In general, the Node-0 sample was distributed across regions and activities.

This project tried to minimize the problems usually associated with snowball sampling by selecting multiple individuals as the starting points rather than a single individual.

---

[43] This probably reflects some selection bias based on perceived threats or challenges among U.S. and international regulators. In particular, individuals involved in illicit activity in Africa are underrepresented in the study. This is not meant to imply that Africa is free of illicit activities, but it is more so reflective of the information sources and the historical emphasis of the law enforcement community.

In a sense, each of the snowballs began rolling with a major transnational smuggler at its center. Using the data on known associates, the team generated a social network that incorporated the associates of each major figure (first degree connections) and the associates of those associates (second degree connections). The forty individuals who served as the departure points were connected to 754 individuals in total. Repeating the same process of mapping the connections for those 754 individuals added another 1,942 individuals to the network.[44] This process is reflected in Figure 2.

Figure 2: Network Construction

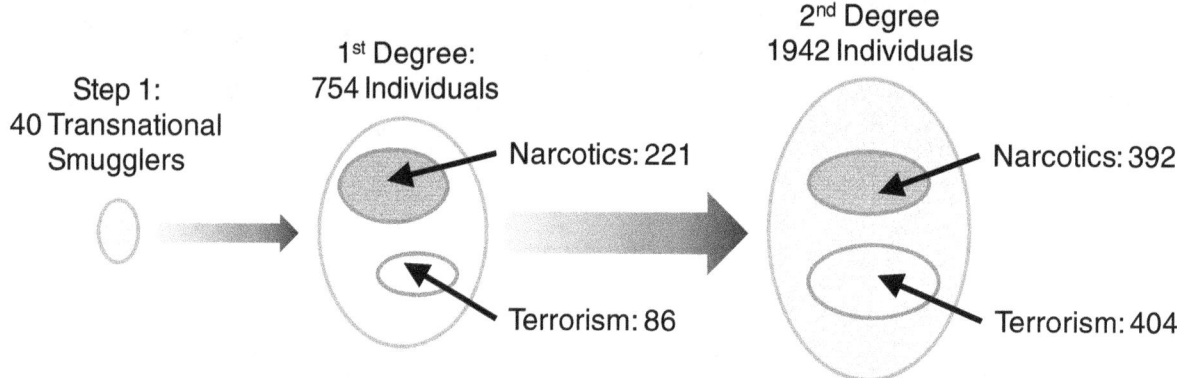

Figure 2 shows how the network sample evolved and also provides a sense of the representation across two different categories of interest: terrorism and narcotics. As previously stated, the 40 transnational smugglers who served as the departure points were connected to 754 individuals. Of that group, 86 had been coded as terrorists and 221 had been coded as being involved in narcotics. There was little surprise that major transnational crime figures would have more criminal than terrorist connections, but those 86 individuals still represent 15 percent of the connections.

---

[44] Identifying a "tie" between two individuals in any such study is difficult. In this study, most information regarding ties was taken from legal filings such as court indictments and sanction designations. While it is possible for legal authorities to identify a known associate through a single transaction, it is more likely that law enforcement identify an associate through a pattern of activity or a regular interaction. Identifying a single, one-off interaction is difficult, and thus ties here are more likely to reflect patterns of interaction.

Also as previously stated, the 754 individuals in the first degree connected to a further 1,942 individuals. Among that group, the number of terrorists spiked sharply, rising to 404, compared with 392 individuals involved in the illegal narcotics business. The number of terrorists increased by 370 percent compared with the growth rates of 158 percent and 77 percent for the entire network and the number of illegal narcotics smugglers respectively.

The final component leveraged for this analysis was the geographic distribution of the actors in the illicit networks. The individuals who formed the basis of this study operated or participated in illicit activities across 122 countries spanning almost every continent. Approximately one third of the people in this study operated in more than one country, with some moving among as many as ten different countries. There are some actors whose locations were simply identified as unknown; however, this represents only about 5 percent of the sample.

The next section of the paper will review the empirical results from the snowball sampling, focusing first on the structure of the social network and then examining the activities and locations of those in the network.

The Connected Dark Network

The starting points for this study and the construction of this sample network were forty internationally prominent transnational smugglers who made their fortunes moving products across national boundaries in violation of domestic or international laws. Smuggling can include moving ostensibly legal items in ways that violate laws on transportation across boundaries or subverting tariffs. That said, most of the individuals in this study were in the business of trafficking in the illicit narcotics trade. A smaller number of individuals were involved in arms dealing. The arms dealers were in the business of selling items that may have been legal, but in many cases they forged end-user certificates to funnel arms to prohibited countries or groups.

Although almost all of these forty kingpins were involved in the transport and sale of illegal items, many of them were also involved in moving legal items illegally, such as making bulk cash transfers. Many of the individuals made the list owing to their primary business, but narcotics dealers are often involved in moving shipments of arms to stock their personnel, and arms dealers might be involved in shipping narcotics for preferred customers or accepting them as a form of payment. Many of these actors might also deal in items like conflict diamonds or counterfeit goods to launder the proceeds from other businesses.

Figure 3: Distinguishing Parallel and Connected Networks

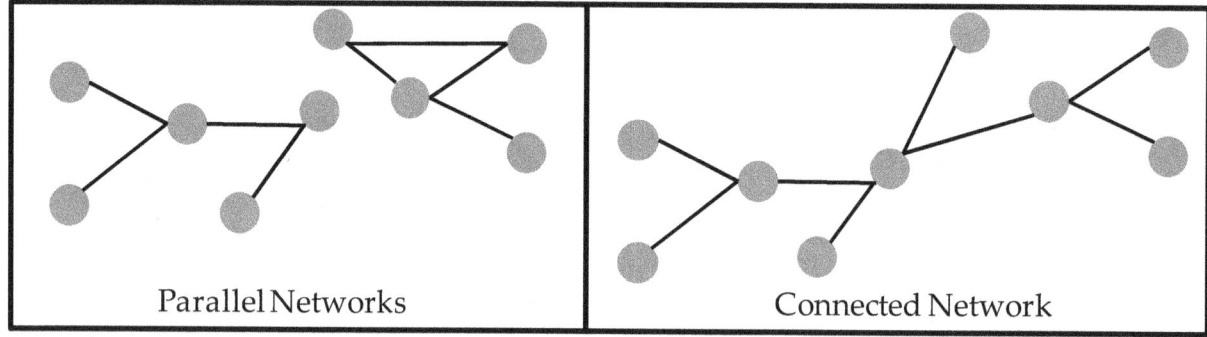

| Parallel Networks | Connected Network |

It may be reasonable to assume or to predict a modest degree of interconnectivity based on illicit market segments and geographic proximity. One could predict that narcotics smugglers in Afghanistan or South Asia would be part of the same network, and that those involved in the Latin American narcotics trade would be connected in parallel network, as shown in Figure 3. This reasoning led to a prediction that the forty smugglers would be distributed across a series of parallel networks based on their geographic centers of gravity and the nature of their illicit activities.

Analyzing Connectivity and Social Distance

The results of the mapping experiment, when the network was completed, were surprising to say the least. The parallel networks very quickly converged into an almost fully connected system. Narcotics smugglers in South Asia were linked to narcotics smugglers in Latin America, and were often separated by only a single degree or relationship. These individuals might be connected by narcotics smugglers in North America, terrorists in Africa, arms dealers in Eastern Europe or financial criminals in Western Europe or in offshore safe havens. In many cases, individuals were linked by multiple relationships. Figure 4 shows how the network developed, beginning with the initial list of transnational smugglers (window 4a), progressing to the 754 first degree connections (window 4b) and finally showing the full sample of individuals (window 4c).

At the outset of the mapping exercise, there was a high possibility of parallel networks, as predicted by the research team and much of the existing literature. As displayed in Figure 4a, at the outset of the study there was one connected group of ten individuals and three smaller components that were each comprised of two individuals who worked with each other.[45] The remaining sample, which included more than 50 percent of the original list, were unconnected to other kingpins or to top smugglers.

It would be reasonable to assume that many of these individuals run networks that might remain unconnected, if for no other reasons than concerns regarding operational security, thus giving rise to parallel networks of illicit activity. This expectation collapses by moving a mere step further to include the known associates of the kingpins.

---

[45] The ten individuals who were connected were largely involved in the Mexican drug trade, with a few operating out of Colombia. Historically, the Colombians have supplied the Mexican criminal organizations with cocaine, and the Mexicans have been responsible for smuggling the product into the United States. This explains the high-level connectivity between individuals in Mexico and Colombia. Within Mexico, criminal organizations have splintered over time, and some of the kingpins in the network under study are connected given those past relationships or associations.

Figure 4: Evolution of Network Map

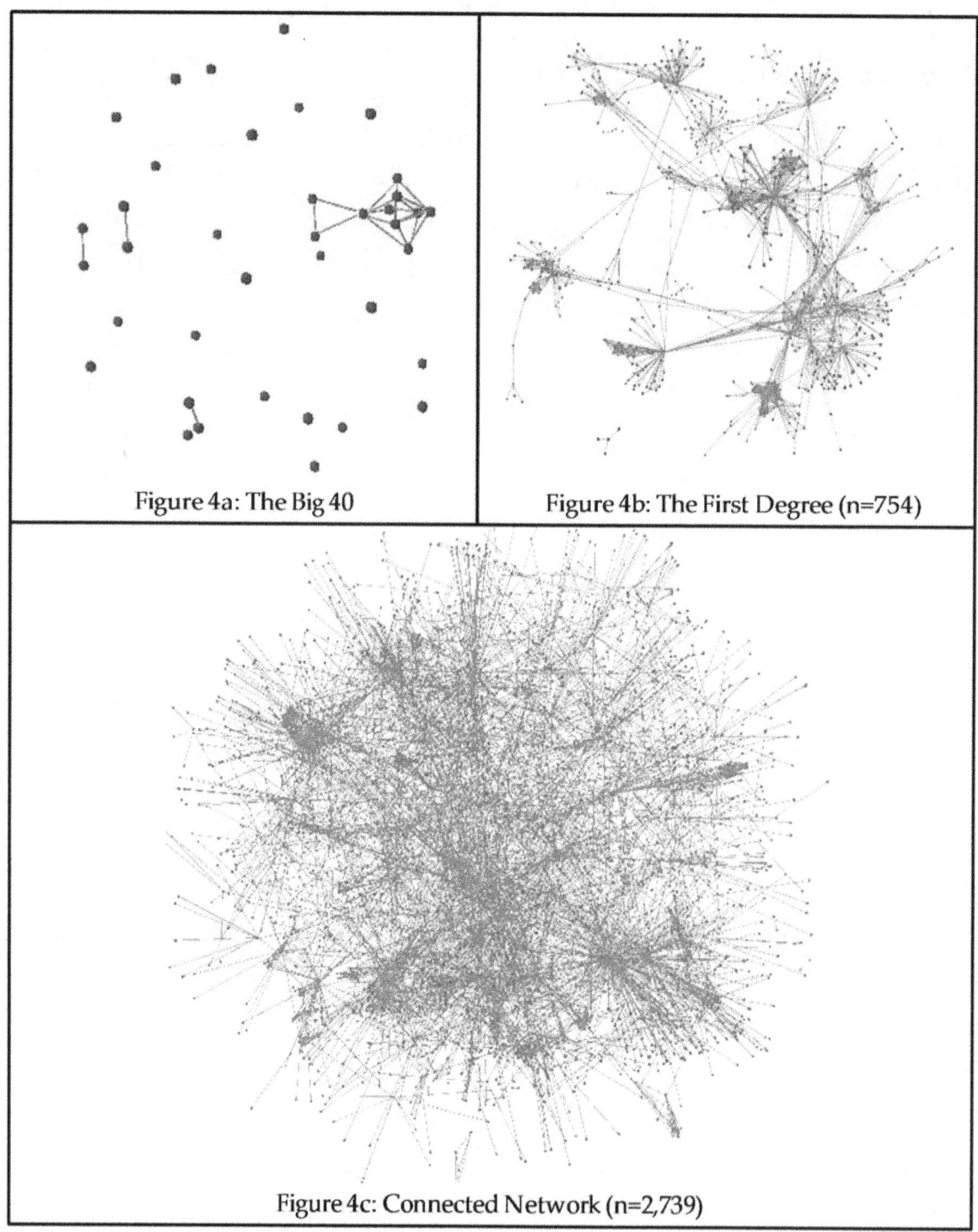

Figure 4a: The Big 40

Figure 4b: The First Degree (n=754)

Figure 4c: Connected Network (n=2,739)

Figure 4b shows that the vast majority of the unconnected individuals in Figure 4a are actually linked together by common associations. There are nine components, meaning nine parallel networks, as opposed to the twenty-six separate components in Figure 4a. Seven of those independent networks, when summed together, include a mere thirty individuals, most in cells of two or three. The second-largest subnetwork includes thirty-nine individuals. Almost seven hundred individuals are subsumed within the largest of the parallel networks. This seven-hundred-person cluster is often referred to in this study as the "giant component." Rather than observing growth among separate parallel networks, connectivity across the subnetworks increased significantly. Approximately 85 percent of the individuals, with just one degree of separation, are part of a single network with a global reach.

The existence of parallel networks collapses almost entirely when the next step of known associates, often called the second degree of separation, is mapped out. It is not uncommon for parallel networks in licit professional communities to converge at three or four steps, but the connectivity usually applies within particular industry sectors like academia, finance or technology.[46] This leads to an interesting insight. Rather than distinguish among different types of illegal businesses, a common social infrastructure across different products helps undergird the global illicit market, encompassing illegal narcotics dealers, arms dealers, organized criminals and terrorists.

The second degree network includes more than 2,700 individuals in eight parallel components, or unconnected networks. The fascinating part is that the second-largest of these parallel networks consists of merely eighteen people. The third- and fourth-largest parallel networks consist of nine and eight people respectively. The rest of these smaller networks include only four or five people. That means only 53 individuals out of the total 2,739 were unconnected to the larger network. Approximately 98.1 percent of the individuals were part of the connected network, separated by a single associate (first degree) or an associate of an associate (second degree).

It is important to recognize that a graph connected by two degrees of relationships does not mean that everyone in the network has access to all others through one or two individuals. Two degrees of connectivity was sufficient to link 98 percent of the

---

[46] M. E. J. Newman, "The structure of scientific collaboration networks," *PNAS* 98, no. 2 (16 January 2001), 404–409. For a contrary assessment see Judith S. Kleinfeld, "Could It Be A Big World After All? The "Six Degrees Of Separation" Myth," Society 2002.

individuals operating across functional domains and geographies, but many of them may be quite socially distant. Figure 5 helps to illustrate this idea. Everyone in the network is connected by two degrees, but individual A has to leverage two other nodes in the network (B and C) before reaching D. The figure also displays the concept of the "shortest path." The analysis below refers to the geodesic distance, or the shortest path, between any two nodes in the network. In this instance the shortest path between individuals A and E is through B and C, bypassing D. If C and E were not connected, then the path would have to travel through D, and as a result would be one link longer.

Figure 5: Example of Connectivity, Social Distance and Path Length

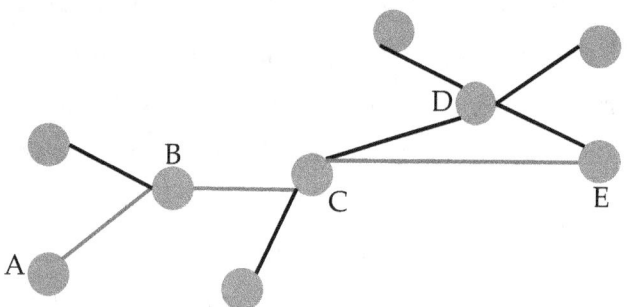

Figure 6 helps to shed light on the nature of the connectivity of the global illicit network mapped and studied here. The graph in Figure 6a shows the distribution of connectivity within the network. More than half the participants (1,676) link to only a single individual. This is not uncommon in many networks. Studies across the social and biological sciences suggest that many networks are characterized by a large number of actors with relatively few connections, say one or two, and a smaller number of well-connected nodes.[47] Thus, the fact of a large number of individuals with a single link to the illicit marketplace is not surprising. The nature of the data collection process may also have inflated that number, since the network mapping stopped at participants two degrees removed from the initial forty individuals. Mapping out an additional series of relationships would reduce the number of individuals with a single connection to the network.

---

[47] Albert-László Barabási, *Linked: How Everything Is Connected to Everything Else and What It Means for Business, Science, and Everyday Life* (New York: Plume Books, 2003).

Figure 6: Network Connectivity Characteristics

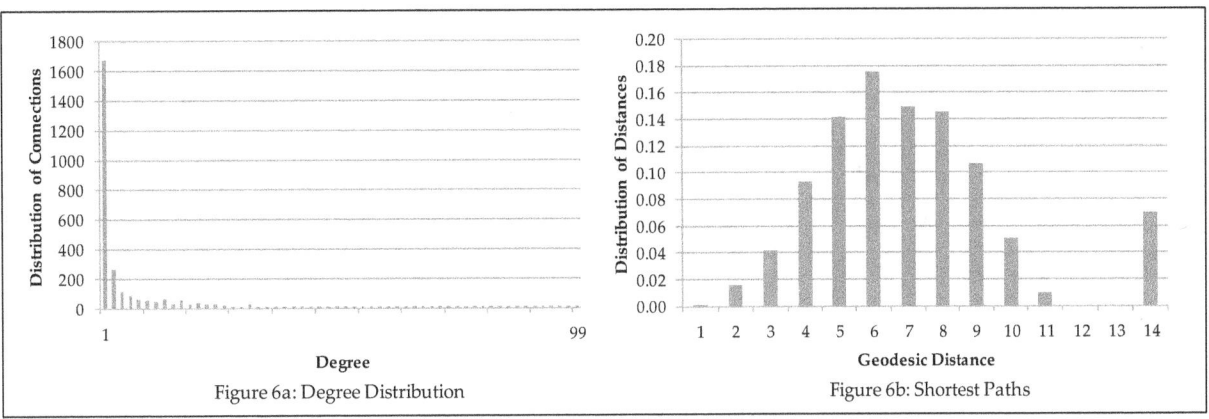

Figure 6a: Degree Distribution   Figure 6b: Shortest Paths

Although the distribution of connections in the network studied here is consistent with that of studies of network structure across many other fields, it does differ in some important ways. An examination of the path length needed to move between any two individuals, often called the geodesic or social distance, suggests that the vast majority of individuals must travel through four to nine other individuals for an introduction.[48] As mentioned above, the network may be almost fully connected in a single giant component by looking at the associates of associates, but almost 8 percent of participants would have to connect through as many as fourteen other participants before getting an introduction (see Figure 6b). Only about 3 percent of the network could reach anyone directly or through an associate. The presence of large path lengths also reveals something important about structure that serves as a slight deviation from many other networks. In particular, this network does not exhibit small-world characteristics, such as the ability of individuals who are not neighbors to still reach each other by going through a very small number of people.

Studies of network science across disciplines often find a hub-and-spoke or scale-free structure, which is characterized by a few very well-connected individuals and many peripheral others. Often these networks follow an 80-20 rule, meaning that 80 percent of the connections are held by 20 percent of the participants.[49] This type of hub-and-spoke structure often explains the efficiency through which materials and information pass

---

[48] Stephen P. Borgatti, "Centrality and Network Flow," *Social Networks* 27, no. 1 (January 2005), 55–71.

[49] Albert-László Barabási, 2003.

through such a network, since the relatively well-connected can move things to participants in relatively few steps. This is why Internet search engines became so important as the Internet grew. Search engines filled the role of a well-connected hub, efficiently moving users to the information they wanted.

The existence of long path lengths (a path length of seven or more) in the network studied here suggests that there is a shortage of hubs in the global illicit network as a whole. An analysis of the Lorenz curves associated with the network shows that it falls short of meeting an 80-20 rule.[50] Approximately 20 percent of the participants account for 65 percent of the connections. While this still has some of the characteristics of a hub-and-spoke network, it reflects either the absence of a few superconnected individuals or a shortage of modestly connected individuals. The network does not meet the normal qualifications for scale-free or small world classification. This network structure may be driven by the clandestine aspect of the network members' activities; however, the same logic generated the earlier faulty expectation of parallel networks.

Although the details of network analysis may seem esoteric at first, they actually reveal some insights with significant national security policy implications. The network may experience inefficiencies in moving materials and information between distant parts despite its connectivity. Those who link these disparate groups are particularly important in this process, and this network has a number of people who can serve such a function. That said, despite the importance of the individuals who link groups together, this analysis suggests that the distribution of relationships is such that it is difficult to disrupt the activities of the global network by targeting a few kingpins. Removing enough of these individuals from the network could break it into disparate parts, but such an outcome assumes that replacements or substitutes are not waiting in the wings.

Such a strategy would work best if there were few hyperconnected individuals in a network, but the relative shortage of these superconnectors in the network studied here

---

[50] Mark Newman, "Power Laws, Pareto Distributions and Zipf's Law," *Contemporary Physics* 46, (2005), 323–351. A Lorenz curve is a way of graphically representing a cumulative probability distribution and helps to identify the presence or absence of a concentration of connections across a part of the population.

means that it is likely to withstand their removal.[51] In other words, there are redundant connections built into the network. This of course is based only on an assessment of the network's structure, and it is important to consider additional insights drawn from incorporating activities and geographic location.

Illicit Activity and Geographic Reach

The graphic in Figure 4c provides one possible snapshot of the illicit network, one in which all of the participants are treated as though they were the same. Of course, they are in fact far from homogenous. The network here includes terrorists, narcotics smugglers, arms dealers, organized criminals, political criminals and suspicious individuals. This coding introduces the possibility of variation across these different topologies within the network. It is possible that these groups, despite being connected in the network, are quite segregated. This would be consistent with many of the arguments that question convergence.[52] These different illicit industries may occasionally work together through intermediaries, but their separation may be the reason behind the social distance discussed above.

The data here are amenable to addressing just such an issue. By color-coding the different nodes in the network based on the illicit activity with which they are associated, the relative degree of segregation and convergence can be explored. A high degree of segregation would be marked by a network with patches of different colors in distinct areas. For example, all the terrorists, colored red, might reside in the upper right, while purple narcotics smugglers would exist in the upper left and organized criminals in the lower right. However, Figure 7 provides little evidence of segregation.

The network in Figure 7 seems to reflect a reasonable degree of convergence between terrorists and those involved in other types of illicit activity. The visual evidence suggests that terrorists are distributed throughout the network. In some cases, there might be one or two individuals involved in terrorist activity subsumed in criminal

---

[51] For a similar finding in terrorist networks, see Scott Helfstein and Dominick Wright, "Covert or Convenient? Evolution of Terror Attack Networks," *Journal of Conflict Resolution* 55 (2011), 785–813.
[52] Naylor, 2002.

networks, but in other cases there are large clusters of terrorists with multiple connections to criminals.

Figure 7: Network with Activities

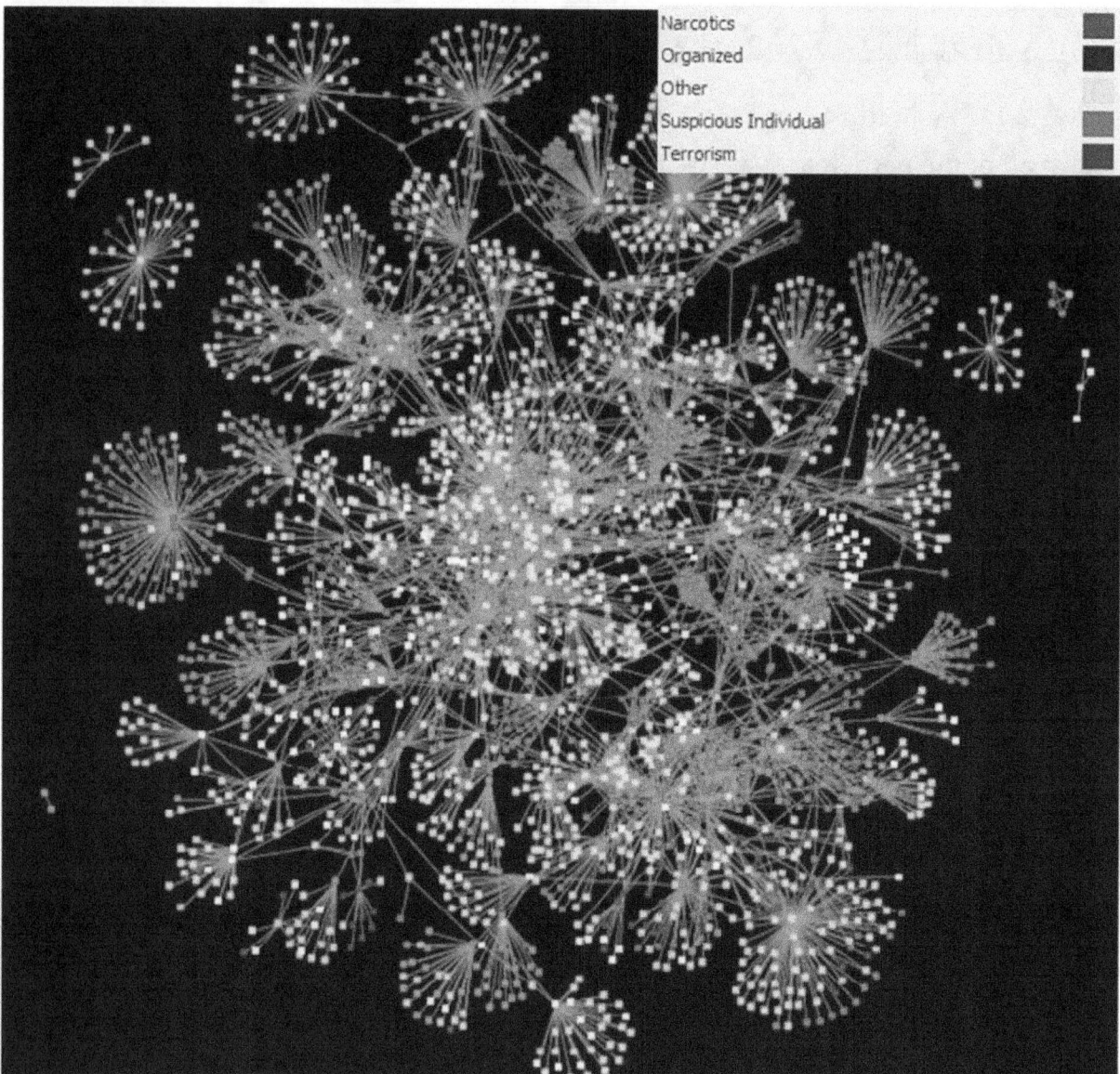

An empirical analysis of this network shows that 46 percent of terrorists' connections are linked to those involved in activities other than terrorism. Some portion of those links are with suspicious individuals, who may over time be designated as a terrorist. At present, however, these suspicious individuals are not designated as terrorists by any governmental body and are therefore incorporated into the statistic above.

Individuals involved in other illicit activities link to terrorists 35 percent of the time. This statistic is telling, since it challenges the conventional wisdom that most criminals eschew relationships with terrorists to avoid drawing the ire of national and international authorities. Almost 20 percent of all the identified connections cross between the criminal-terrorist boundary, and more than one-third of criminals' social connections tie to terrorists. Terrorists are most likely to connect with narcotics traffickers, representing over 40 percent of the cross-functional links. This is followed by links with suspicious individuals, political criminals and financial criminals. Terrorists are also a party to 43 percent of the total social connections in the network, which indicates that they are prominent social connectors. Their relations are not restrained to fellow terrorists, since those links only account for 54 percent of terrorists' connections.

Table 2 shows the summary statistics across individuals involved in different activities. One interesting finding is that this network is saturated with almost as many terrorists as those involved in narcotics, and the number of those involved in terrorism significantly outweighs the number of those involved in organized crime and other types of criminality. That is a significant finding, since the initial building blocks of the inquiry were all criminals. Despite the initial focus on transnational smuggling, the network is nonetheless populated with a large number of people designated as terrorists.

Table 2: Summary Statistics by Illicit Activity

Activity	Individuals	Average Countries	Average Degree	Average Betweenness	Average Closeness
Narcotics	633	1.34	5.941	0.502	0.959
Organized	77	1.30	2.973	0.125	0.918
Other	121	1.25	2.934	0.044	0.867
Political	68	1.20	3.426	0.129	0.959
Suspicious Individual	1343	1.18	3.015	0.055	0.919
Terrorism	497	1.65	4.881	0.204	0.962
Total	2739	1.30	4.037	0.189	0.935

The table also shows the existence of some substantive structural differences across individuals based upon their activities. The average individual in the network is connected to four others, but those involved in narcotics and terrorism are substantially more connected than the others. The average degree measure shows that those involved with narcotics have the highest average connectivity, as measured by degree, with such individuals linking to almost six others, followed by terrorists with an average connectivity score of almost five. Interestingly, members of organized criminal groups and other criminals were on the low end of the connectivity scale.

The number of connections an individual has is the most common way of conceptualizing connectivity and network structure, but there are a number of other measures frequently utilized in the study of large networks. One is betweenness. Those with high betweenness scores link disparate parts of a network, which has led some to describe the role of these people as boundary spanners.[53] These are individuals who are part of different cliques, in the casual sense, and their presence in many groups is critical to the connectivity and flow of ideas or material through a network. In the illicit world, individuals with high betweenness are those like Ilyas Kashmiri, Monzer al-Kassar and Victor Bout, who connect with people from different social spheres around the world.[54]

Those involved in the narcotics trade have the highest average betweenness scores, and, surprisingly, terrorists have the second-highest average. This further challenges the idea that others in the illicit world eschew terrorists because of their stigma or the related security concerns. The analytics here suggest that terrorists actually play a reasonably important role in linking disparate cells and groups to one another. Individuals involved in the illegal drug trade and terrorism are the most likely boundary spanners. Terrorists often have to broker connections with a range of individuals to undertake

---

[53] Linton C. Freeman, "A Set of Measures of Centrality Based on Betweenness," *Sociometry* 40, no. 1 (March 1977), 35–41.

[54] Each of these individuals has a unique story behind his connectivity, and only a short description will be offered here. Ilyas Kashmiri is a militant from South Asia who has been a member of or worked with relationships with Harkat-ul-Jihad al-Islami (Huji), LeT, al-Qai'da and D-Company, which gave him a breadth of connections to link groups in regional militant landscape. Monzer al-Kassar and Victor Bout were both arms dealers. Bout rose to prominence by selling excess Soviet arms after the Cold War and his business network crossed every continent. Kassar also had ties with Eastern European arms dealers, and he sold weapons in the Middle East, Africa and South America. These types of individuals link disparate groups.

successful attacks, and this may help to explain this connectivity. Political criminals and suspicious individuals fall in the middle, with organized criminals and other criminal figures tending toward isolation. This finding suggests that organized crime is relatively disciplined in limiting its connectivity to other groups, but the same cannot be said for other types of illicit actors and organizations.

Another way of thinking about connectivity uses a measure called closeness, which examines how many links one must travel through to reach other members of a given network. [55] The higher one's score, the closer an individual is socially to everyone else, making it easier for him or her to connect with others or to funnel resources. Unlike the betweenness scores, which show some significant deviation in our study, the average closeness scores of the six groups are relatively similar. Terrorists are actually the closest to others in the network, followed by those involved in narcotics and political crime. Criminals classified as "other" had the lowest score, but the difference between the highest and lowest scores was less than 0.1.

The measures of connectivity can also be combined to understand the roles that individuals involved in different activities may play in the network. Figure 8 combines two measures, betweenness and Eigenvector centralities. Betweenness, as mentioned above, helps identify people who link different cliques or otherwise isolated parts of the network. These people can be thought of as brokers who can facilitate activities across different groups and potentially distant parts of the network. Those with high Eigenvector scores are generally connected to others who are in turn well-connected. One need not have a lot of connections to have a high Eigenvector score; rather, it is more important for one's connections to be well-connected. Those with high Eigenvector scores are generally thought of as gatekeepers. These nodes help others access highly connected individuals. Those who score highly using both metrics can be thought of as superbrokers or superconnectors.

The topology in Figure 8 recasts some of the assumptions about crime-terror connectivity, specifically the idea that terrorists are likely to play a marginal role. While

---

[55] Timothy J. Rowley, "Moving beyond Dyadic Ties: A Network Theory of Stakeholder Influences," *Academy of Management Review* 22, no. 4 (October 1997), 887–910.

this network has seven superbrokers, all of whom are narcotics traffickers, terrorists are disproportionately represented as brokers in the network as well. A subset of the terrorists in the network play an important role in connecting disparate groups. By contrast, terrorist actors did not typically link to well-connected individuals. The gatekeepers were more likely to be narcotics traffickers and suspicious individuals. Suspicious individuals, in particular, are likely to make good gatekeepers by adding a sense of legitimacy to the well-connected individuals with whom they work. The vast majority of the individuals in the network are peripheral players, according to the dividing lines above.

Figure 8: Categorizing Connectivity

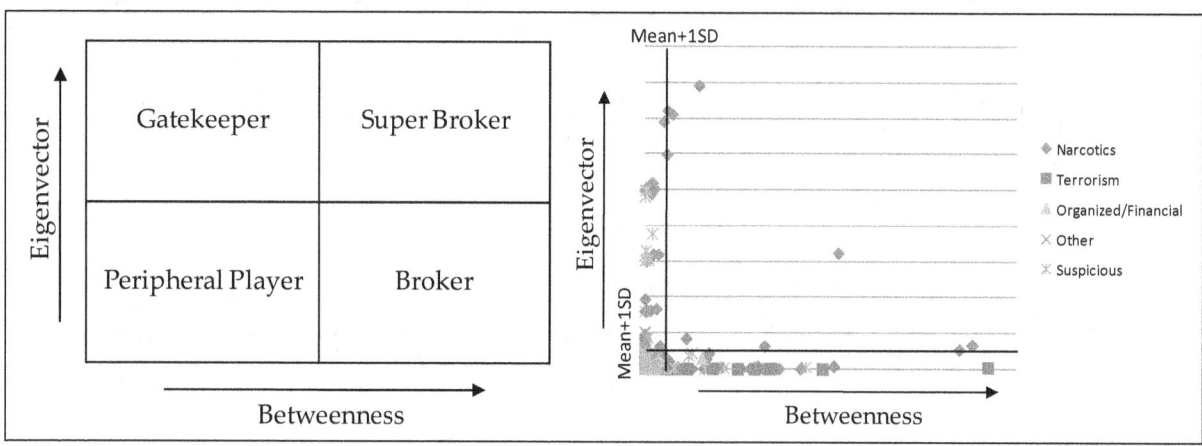

The network analytics suggests that terrorists are no more or less operationally secure than many other criminals are. They are deeply imbedded in the larger criminal network, they span boundaries to link otherwise separate clusters or organizations and they are relatively close to others in the network. These results may be interpreted to suggest that the most effective means of countering such a global illicit network involves a mixture of the tools used to counter criminal activity with those used to counter terrorism.

In terms of geography, the network under study spans 122 countries, and there are some interesting aspects associated with connectivity across the globe. Figure 9 offers a visual assessment of intercountry connectivity. While one could generate a geospatial network analysis of individuals, the sheer size of the network, with more than 2,700 people operating in 3,600 places linked by 15,000 connections, the resulting map would be blacked out by lines. Instead, Figure 9 summarizes the transnational relationships by looking at which countries have illicit connections to other countries based on the social network developed here. The node markers for each country are placed in the middle of their territorial boundaries (center-mass), and the results show the global reach of the network in this study. In total, the network contains more than 1,000 country-to-country relationships spanning the globe.

Figure 9: Country Connectivity

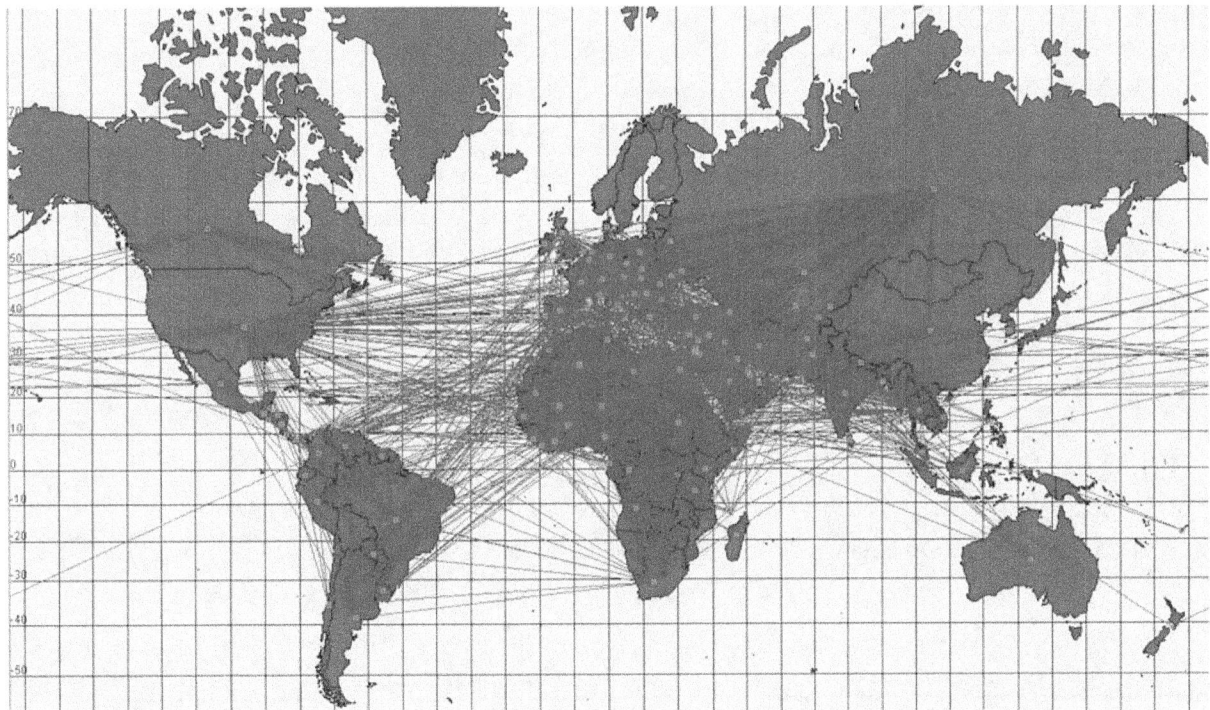

This visual evidence reflects an interconnected transnational network, but it simplifies relationships by looking only at the country-to-country connections and by ignoring the strength of the connections. One way of thinking about this strength is by looking at the frequency of cross-border connections at an individual level, which in turn provides a measure of frequency. Table 3 shows the most common bilateral illicitly linked countries, and it contains some interesting patterns. The criminal links into the United States from the traditional drug-producing and -trafficking countries in the Western hemisphere tops the list. The United States is the largest market for illicit narcotics and the ties are extensive. Below that, there are a number of relationships that link countries in South Asia and the Middle East, with a particular emphasis on countries traditionally

47

used for transit, like the United Arab Emirates. Further down, the connections get more diverse, linking Europe, South America, South Asia, the Middle East and North America.

Table 3: Top Bilateral Illicit Connections

Rank	Country	Rank	Country
1	Mexico - USA	20	India - Portugal
2	Colombia - USA	21	Guatemala - Mexico
3	India - United Arab Emirates	22	India - Kenya
4	India - Pakistan	23	Nigeria - India
5	Colombia - Mexico	24	Sudan - Pakistan
6	Pakistan - United Arab Emirates	25	Spain - Syria
7	Afghanistan - Pakistan	26	Saudi Arabia - Sudan
8	India - Thailand	27	United Arab Emirates - USA
9	Colombia - Panama	28	India - Nepal
10	India - Malaysia	29	France - Syria
11	Colombia - Venezuela	30	Argentina - Syria
12	India - USA	31	Russian Federation - United Arab Emirates
13	Korea, South - USA	32	Russian Federation - USA
14	India - Mali	33	Afghanistan - USA
15	Afghanistan - Saudi Arabia	34	Liberia - Russian Federation
16	Pakistan - Saudi Arabia	35	Canada - India
17	Pakistan - USA	36	Russian Federation - South Africa
18	Venezuela - USA	37	Belgium - Russian Federation
19	Afghanistan - Sudan	38	Guatemala - USA

To look at the list above can be instructive, but it can also be deceiving. The list focuses on the most common bilateral links, but assessing the raw number of connections may not be the best way to assess the network's overall connectivity. This is where more powerful statistical techniques can be helpful in understanding complex networks. Although the visual and analytical evidence above shows a high level of connectivity within the network as a whole as well as among criminals and terrorists, it does not satisfactorily explain why this connectivity is higher than one might predict. This is the task of the next section, which will examine some competing hypotheses about crime-terror connectivity.

1992

Dawood Ibrahim controlled an underworld empire based in India when race riots broke out in that country in 1992, claiming the lives of an estimated 1,200 Muslims. Many, Ibrahim included, blamed the Indian government and what they considered to have been an inadequate effort to protect the Muslim victims.[56] The riots, however, were not the only issue that occupied Ibrahim's thoughts that year. D-Company, an underworld organization built by Ibrahim, was undergoing a transition. Many of the smuggling businesses that had been so lucrative for the organization early on, chief among them the gold smuggling business, had come under pressure as Indian prime minister P. V. Narasimha Rao continued to remove the tariffs and restrictions that had fueled the Indian illicit marketplace.[57]

The shrinking black market, and the pressure to move into ever more dangerous and illicit activities, created tremendous tension in the Indian criminal underworld.[58] From his perch in Dubai, Ibrahim developed a plan that would both exact revenge on the Indian government he saw culpable in the race riots as well as strike out at his underworld competitors.[59] By late 1992, Ibrahim's lieutenants were training would-be bombers and coordinating logistics for the March 1993 Bombay attack, which involved thirteen bombs placed in the heart of the city's business district. Ibrahim and his D-Company would send a message to the government and competitors alike, using the medium of civilian causalities.[60]

From his European headquarters, Monzer al-Kassar had other concerns at the time. The Syrian-born smuggler had been moving illicit materials of all kinds since his work with Eastern European intelligence agencies began in the early 1980s, when he gained particular prominence in the field of arms smuggling.[61] While the arms trade is a large

---

[56] Clarke and Lee, 2008.

[57] Glenny, 2008.

[58] Ibid.

[59] Rollins and Wyler, 2010.

[60] Gregory F. Treverton et al., *Film Piracy, Organized Crime, and Terrorism*, RAND Corporation, 2009, 121

[61] Interview with special agent from the Drug Enforcement Administration, July 2012.

and licit business around the world, some arms dealers choose to pursue larger profits by supplying governments or nonstate actors that are explicitly barred from purchasing arms through legitimate channels. The people engaged in this illicit side business justify high prices and huge profit margins given the risks they incur. This is what occupied al-Kassar in 1992 as he negotiated arms deals with Bosnia, Croatia and Somalia in violation of United Nations sanctions.[62]

The deals netted him millions of dollars, but he was not able to enjoy the fruits of his labor for long. In September 1992, the Spanish government arrested al-Kassar for his suspected involvement in the *Achille Lauro* hijacking. He would go on to spend a year in prison before being released, and he would be acquitted in a Spanish court two years later.[63] From his home base in Marbella, Spain, al-Kassar resumed business as usual, acting as one of the world's leading arms dealers, supplying rogue regimes and terrorists alike.[64]

While Ibrahim was plotting his attack and al-Kassar was negotiating his arms agreements, Mohamad Youssef Hammoud arrived in New York City with forged travel documents during 1992.[65] Hammoud was a loyal member of the Iranian- and Syrian-backed group gaining power in southern Lebanon called Hezbollah. Hammoud was not sent to New York to conduct a terrorist attack but rather to develop a new source of financial support. Hammoud was an enterprising individual who quickly established a

---

[62] The Bosnia and Croatia sales are detailed in Matthew Brunwasser, "Monzer Al Kassar: The Prince of Marbella: Arms to All Sides," *Frontline*, available at www.pbs.org/frontlineworld/stories/sierraleone/alkassar.html; for reference to Somalia, see Richard Greenberg, "The Godfather of Terror," NBC News, August 2010, available at www.nbcnews.com/id/38489721/ns/dateline_nbc-international/t/godfather-terror/#.UlW3slODmSo.
[63] Greenberg, 2010.
[64] Patrick Radden Keefe, "The Trafficker: The Decades-Long Battle to Catch an International Arms Broker," *The New Yorker*, 8 February 2010, available at www.newyorker.com/reporting/2010/02/08/100208fa_fact_keefe.
[65] Immigration and Customs Enforcement, "News Release: Mohamad Youssef Hammoud sentenced to 30 years in terrorism financing case," 27 July 2011, available at www.ice.gov/news/releases/1101/110127charlotte.htm.

network of licit and illicit enterprises that included a gas station funded with a fraudulently obtained $1.6 million loan from the U.S. Small Business Administration.[66]

Hammoud's crown jewel was a cigarette smuggling enterprise that authorities believed netted $8 million by the time it was disrupted in 2002, with much of its proceeds finding their way back to Hezbollah's coffers in Lebanon.[67] The year 1992, as it would turn out, was pivotal not only for Hammoud but also for Hezbollah. That year, the group decided to participate in Lebanese elections for the first time.[68] It was also the year that Hezbollah would organize and carry out the bombing of the Israeli embassy in Argentina that would kill twenty-three individuals.[69] U.S. law enforcement officials started tracking the activities of Hammoud's gang in 1995 as they made large cigarette purchases.[70] The authorities investigated the group for six years and produced a series of convictions.

There was nothing particularly special about 1992 in the history of illicit business and terrorist activity, which makes the above vignettes all the more interesting. Each represents a different manifestation or evolution of crime and terrorist activity. Hammoud was not sent to the United States to conduct a terrorist attack but rather to raise funds through criminal activity on behalf of the state-sponsored group Hezbollah. This is a classic example of a terrorist group moving into profit-oriented crime to support the organization. At the same time, al-Kassar served as a classic example of a facilitator aiding terrorist groups, rogue regimes and transnational criminal organizations as he saw economically and ideologically fit. And Ibrahim and D-

---

[66] David E. Kaplan, "Homegrown Terrorists: How a Hezbollah Cell Made Millions in Sleepy Charlotte, N.C.," *U.S. News and World Report*, 2 March 2003, available at www.usnews.com/usnews/news/articles/030310/10hez.htm.

[67] Ibid.

[68] Krista E. Wiegand, "Reformation of a Terrorist Group: Hezbollah as a Lebanese Political Party," *Studies in Conflict and Terrorism* 32, no. 8 (2009), 669–680.

[69] Mathew Levitt, "Hezbollah's 1992 Attack in Argentina Is a Warning for Modern-Day Europe," *The Atlantic*, 19 March 2013, available at www.theatlantic.com/international/archive/2013/03/hezbollahs-1992-attack-in-argentina-is-a-warning-for-modern-day-europe/274160/.

[70] Kaplan, 2003.

Company illustrate a criminal organization that moves into terrorist activity with the help of a state sponsor.

Although each of these trajectories is well documented, their patterns do not necessarily explain why or the conditions under which criminality and terrorism converge. Interestingly, none of these cases reflects the typical example of such convergence, involving a failed or impoverished country. In 1992, none of the states in the above anecdotes were classified as failed states. Hammoud set up his criminal enterprise in the United States, hardly a failed state, and he operated on behalf of the Lebanon-based organization Hezbollah, a substate group operating in what at the time was a troubled but relatively wealthy Middle East banking center. The Western European city of Marbella, Spain, from which al-Kassar ran his organization, is hardly a failed state as well. Al-Kassar's clients represent a more mixed picture than those of the previous two men, with some of his clients in the throes of civil wars in failed states, others involved in subversive campaigns against capable governments along with a fair share of sovereign dictators. Ibrahim was operating out of India, hardly a failed state, until he moved to Dubai, a growing and stable frontier market in the Middle East. He would settle in India and maintain a network that transverses much of the region. These examples do not easily represent the resource-constrained cases associated with the failed or impoverished state argument, suggesting a need for further exploration.

Difficulties of Explaining Connectivity

The empirical assessment of the network in this paper suggests that there is a high degree of connectivity among terrorists and criminals, and that relationships between terrorists and other criminals are relatively common. This raises some important questions: Why is connectivity more pronounced than one may have expected? What explains the tendency for criminals and terrorists to work together?

Part of the reason that the high level of connectivity remains underappreciated by many scholars and policy makers lies in the dominant paradigm of convergence. The overlap between criminal and terrorist networks is often perceived as an outlying or rare event. From this perspective, groups are occasionally pushed into sharing resources, profiting off a one-time exchange, transferring knowledge through training resources or borrowing tactics in situations in which the connectivity is limited and short-term. If that really described the nature of these connections, then it would be almost impossible for law enforcement agencies to track these relationships, and they would not turn up in this analysis. The reality, captured in the network analysis described here, is that connectivity occurs with sufficient frequency for law enforcement and the media to document the activities. In most cases, there is mutual benefit gained from maintaining such a relationship, and so crime-terror connectivity becomes a rule rather than an exception.

One way to better understand this is to look beyond the network paradigm. While the mapping exercise focused on the relationships in the network, it also illustrates, perhaps in the most comprehensive fashion yet, the infrastructure of the global illicit marketplace. The connections that link individuals are the paths by which criminals and terrorists move material and ideas. These are the foundations for illicit transactions. Conceptualizing the pattern of relationships as a network and a market helps to provide fresh explanations for connectivity. While explanatory or causal theory in networks is still in many ways in the early stages, theory on markets and economics is well developed. Since the data here represent both a network and a marketplace, there may be opportunity to provide a richer set of causal explanations by leveraging ideas from both fields.

Conventional Explanation: Research Scarcity in Failed or Poor States

It is important to examine the underlying reasons that crime-terror links develop. Although activity appropriation and organizational cooperation are manifestations of connectivity, neither provides a causal explanation for the behavior. This lack of causal explanation is a common attribute of the literature, which focuses more on documenting the manifestations of connectivity rather than looking for systemic explanations of it. The "motives not means" perspective pushes this forward, encouraging analysts to look at what people do and why.

The most common explanation for crime-terror connectivity focuses on resource scarcity in failed or poor states (called "resource scarcity" for short). This explanation was featured in a recent Department of Defense white paper that argued, "Weak and unstable government institutions coupled with scarce legitimate economic opportunities, extreme socio-economic inequities, and permissive corrupt environments

53

are key enablers that allow TCOs to operate with impunity. These same factors enable the emergence of violent extremist organizations (VEOs)."[71] The two-part causal argument here is straightforward. First, weak and unstable governments struggle to combat threats within their borders, including crime and terrorism. These illicit forces can operate, on their own or in conjunction, with a degree of impunity given the absence of domestic institutions capable of countering them. Second, the poverty or deprivation present in such environments drives individuals looking for income toward the comparatively lucrative areas of illicit activity.

Challenging Conventional Wisdom

While this argument continues to dominate conventional wisdom, there are a number of underlying assumptions that need to be examined. Working backward, the first assumption to explore is that poverty or poor economic conditions drives people into the illicit sectors. While this seems reasonable on its merits, it is actually a very controversial notion.[72] Empirically, many studies have actually found that crime rates rose as societies' economies grew.[73] Citizens in cities like São Paulo and Mexico City experienced increases in criminal activity during significant economic expansions. Those who oppose the poverty-crime argument suggest that economic growth offers new and growing illicit markets that attract customers, whereas the illicit market in poor societies is capped in a sense.[74] Arguments about crime and poverty also often conflate two issues: poverty and inequality. It might be that inequality, which is more apparent in economically growing and wealthy environments, is a more salient driver for criminal activity.[75] While this paper will not attempt to settle this complicated debate, it is important to recognize that poverty or "scarce legitimate economic

---

[71] Cabayan, 2013.

[72] Kristin M. Finklea, "Economic Downturns and Crime," Congressional Research Service, 19 December 2011, available at www.fas.org/sgp/crs/misc/R40726.pdf.

[73] Francois J. Bourguignon, "Crime as a Social Cost of Poverty and Inequality: A Review Focusing on Developing Countries," *Revista Desarrollo y Sociedad* (September 1999), 61–99.

[74] Ibid.

[75] E. Britt Patterson, "Poverty, Income Inequality, and Community Crime Rates," *Criminology* 29, no. 4 (November 1991) 755–776; Morgan Kelly, "Inequality and Crime," *The Review of Economics and Statistics* 82, no. 4 (November 2000), 530–539.

opportunities" in and of itself may not necessarily drive people toward criminal behavior or illicit activities.

The second assumption to examine is the notion that criminal and terrorist actors are most likely to thrive in environments with weak governments and poverty. This, however, is another contentious claim. The absence of a capable government, or so one line of reasoning suggests, means that illicit actors can operate unchecked and grow their enterprises. James Piazza did find that failed states were likely incubators of terrorist activity, but there are also examples of terrorist groups that move out of failed states because of the operating conditions within them.[76] The core of what would become al-Qa'ida left Afghanistan in the early 1990s amid that country's growing civil strife, and the group essentially pulled its operatives off the Horn of Africa later in the 1990s because of the difficult operating environment there.[77] Sunni terror groups, particularly al-Qa'ida, have generally found Lebanon to be an inhospitable place amid its civil strife and ethnic tension.[78] By contrast, groups situated in more stable, developing countries can persist for some time.[79]

For example, Usama bin Ladin referred to South Africa—a stable, growing economy— as an "open territory," and there is a prolonged record of al-Qa'ida elements using the country as a planning, fundraising and staging hub for nearly two decades. There are many examples of threat convergence in South Africa. Locally based organized crime groups, for example, have until recently run a considerable false document business,

---

[76] James A. Piazza, "Incubators of Terror: Do Failed and Failing States Promote Transnational Terrorism?," *International Studies Quarterly* 52, no. 3 (September 2008) 469–488.

[77] lint Watts, Jacob Shapiro, and Vahid Brown, *Al-Qa'ida's (Mis)Adventures in the Horn of Africa* (West Point: Combating Terrorism Center, 2007)

[78] Bilal Y. Saab, "Al-Qa`ida's Presence and Influence in Lebanon," *CTC Sentinel*, November 2008, available at www.ctc.usma.edu/posts/al-qaida%E2%80%99s-presence-and-influence-in-lebanon.

[79] Recidivist groups operating in environments with more wealth tend to survive longer according to S. Brock Blomberg, Rozlyn C. Engel, and Reid Sawyer, "On the Duration and Sustainability of Transnational Terrorist Organizations," *Journal of Conflict Resolution* 54, no. 2 (April 2010), 303–330.

servicing thousands of militant Islamists in transit between South Asia and Europe with fraudulently obtained passports.[80]

Criminals also struggle in weak states with no governance because it is more difficult to make a profit and to protect one's earnings in such an environment. It was difficult for Afghan drug traffickers to operate in the 1990s because there were numerous warlords and gangs demanding transit payoffs along the smuggling routes.[81] The Taliban centralized the system so that traffickers required a single payoff, which made operating in that country easier and allowed traffickers to keep more of their ill-gotten gains. Ironically, the same authorities who make it difficult to earn money in the illicit market also help to protect those gains from others. It is also important to recognize that many criminals have only modest control or decision-making power in the places in which they operate. Illegal narcotics are produced in only a few places, and there is a need for criminals to move their goods out of them and into developed markets in order to make profit. In short, there are both costs and benefits incurred from operating in countries with both weak and strong government institutions.

A third unstated assumption is that a weak government, and the lack of deterrence associated with the absence of a capable law enforcement mechanism, generally opens a space or a sanctuary for terrorists and criminals to cooperate in. In other words, this assumption states that because it is easy for criminals and terrorists to work together, they will. This assumption focuses on the opportunity that is afforded to illicit actors when they operate in environments in which government institutions are incapable of enforcing the law.[82] This, however, also deserves another look. The idea that different groups, particularly criminals and terrorists, would work together just because they can

---

[80] Agiza Hlongwane and Jeff Wicks, "'White Widow' Paid for SA Passport," *IOL*, 29 September 2013, available at http://www.iol.co.za/news/politics/white-widow-paid-for-sa-passport-1.1584186#.U2AIXqLf2K8.

[81] See Ahmed Rashid, *Taliban: Militant Islam, Oil and Fundamentalism in Central Asia* (New Haven: Yale University Press, 2000, second edition).

[82] Louise I. Shelley and John T. Picarelli, "Methods and Motives: Exploring Links between Transnational Organized Crime and International Terrorism," *Trends in Organized Crime* 9, no. 2 (Winter 2005), 52–67.; Ken Menkhaus, "Quasi-States, Nation-Building, and Terrorist Safe Havens," *Journal of Conflict Studies* 23, no. 2 (Fall 2003), available at http://journals.hil.unb.ca/index.php/JCS/article/viewArticle/216/374.

do so with impunity ignores the deeper strategic justifications for such relationships.[83] Criminals, as the logic goes, should particularly loathe working with terrorists when there are capable law enforcement institutions present that can detect such a collaboration and punish the criminals accordingly. Working with terrorists in such an environment is to set up a lightening rod, according to this argument. It does not necessarily stand to reason, however, that the two groups would work together just because criminals have no fear of the law enforcement apparatuses present in weak states. There is a need for a better explanation of what drives the collaboration between criminals and terrorists across different operational environments.

The fourth assumption, also unstated, is that the governmental and illicit actors are adversaries. In the United States, governmental forces bear the responsibility for battling criminal and terrorist elements, and there is an assumption that this adversarial relationship is the rule rather than the exception elsewhere. While the governments of many states do actively combat criminals and terrorists, this is not a universal norm. Counterintuitive to those in Western democracies, there are many instances in which a government and criminals have a cooperative relationship.

There is a large literature on the state sponsorship of terrorism that highlights countries' willingness to support violent substate actors to pursue certain goals.[84] The most obvious examples include Pakistan's support of Lashkar-e-Taybha and Iran's support for Hezbollah, and numerous other examples may be seen throughout history. But although the idea that states might support a terrorist group is fairly well established in the literature, the notion that states may support criminals is less so.

Literature on organized crime has long recognized the importance of political corruption and patron-client relationships that is a centerpiece in a successful organized enterprise. These criminals corrupt the legitimate political system in pursuit of their

---

[83] Naylor, 2002.

[84] Wardlaw, 1987; Meghan L. O'Sullivan, *Shrewd Sanctions: Statecraft and State Sponsors of Terrorism* (Washington: Brookings Institution Press, 2003); Byman, 2005; Navin A. Bapat, "State Bargaining with Transnational Terrorist Groups," *International Studies Quarterly* 50, no. 1 (March 2006), 213–230; David B. Carter, "A Blessing or a Curse? State Support for Terrorist Groups," *International Organization* 66, no. 1 (January 2012), 129–151.

ends, and they have been able to corrupt capable and wealthy governments.[85] Government sponsorship or cultivation of criminal enterprises has not received the same attention. For example, the prominent families atop Russia's political hierarchy often have ties to criminal enterprises alongside their legitimate political and business interests.[86] The government of that country is not pitted against the criminals. Examples from Eastern Europe after the fall of the Soviet Union show how young, weak or economically constrained states can also be co-opted by criminal forces, essentially becoming client states operating in the express interests of criminal elements.[87] Lastly, another permutation has emerged, in which governments actively cultivate the criminal underworld to help the state achieve some national security goal. This is similar to state-sponsored terrorism, and historical examples include those of Serbia and North Korea.[88]

Given the identified weaknesses demonstrated in the four assumptions identified above (and recapitulated in Table 10) tying weak government, poverty and illicit activity to the crime-terror connectivity, there is a need to offer a systemic look at alternative possible explanations. As noted, these assumptions do not necessarily explain why terrorists and criminals may interact in environments that do not provide relative freedom from law enforcement scrutiny. There appears to be a missing element.

Table 4: Four Assumptions in Resource Scarcity Explanation

Assumption 1:	Poverty or poor economic conditions drives people into the illicit sectors.
Assumption 2:	Criminal and terrorist actors are more likely to thrive in environments with weak governments and poverty.
Assumption 3:	Because it is easy for terrorists and criminals to cooperate, they will.
Assumption 4:	Government and illicit actors are adversaries.

[85] For a discussion of political corruption in Seattle, see William Chambliss, *On the Take* (Bloomington, IN: Indiana University Press, 1988)

[86] Fred Burton and Dan Burges, "Russian Organized Crime," *Stratfor*, 17 November 2007 available at www.stratfor.com/weekly/russian_organized_crime.

[87] Gleny, 2008.

[88] Andreas, 2005; Sheena Chestnut, "Illicit Activity and Proliferation: North Korean Smuggling Networks," *International Security* 32, no. 1 (Summer 2007), 80–111.

Terrorists engage in criminal behavior and work with criminal networks, as the logic goes, in order to sustain their group and to access funds, weapons or know-how. One risk to terrorists who engage in criminal activity is the possibility that their political goals and ideological fervor are slowly eroded, and that their group undergoes the transition to a criminal entity. This is how some have explained the trajectory of the FARC in Colombia.[89] Yet it is relatively easy to understand why terrorists may have some interest in criminal activities despite this risk.

The opposite side of the coin has proved far more vexing for those focused on crime-terror convergence. It has been far more difficult to explain why economically motivated criminal groups would be interested in working with terrorists, but the empirical assessment described in this paper suggests that it is commonplace. Conventional wisdom holds that criminal networks are more likely to be punished by national governments if they maintain affiliations with terrorist groups than if they do not. Criminal groups do not want to draw that type of attention to their activities, this wisdom maintains, and these groups do better when they can focus on their pursuit of profit away from the lightening rod of politically motivated terrorist actors. While this paradigm has generally guided strategic thinking on the topic, it draws a potentially artificial divide between the fear that terrorists often exert in their trade of violent political activism and the fear that criminals often use to keep their members in line and law enforcement at arm's length in pursuit of profit. Groups may have learned that cooperation is mutually beneficial over time.[90]

In light of that challenge, it is important to consider a range of alternative explanations.

Alternate Hypotheses

There are four hypotheses aimed at explaining high levels of crime-terror connectivity developed here and empirically tested in the next section. The first of these, resource scarcity, has already been discussed at great length. Three others will be considered below: comparative advantage in competitive environments; terror and crime to

---

[89] Bilal Y. Saab and Alexandra W. Taylor, "Criminality and Armed Groups: A Comparative Study of FARC and Paramilitary Groups in Colombia," *Studies in Conflict and Terrorism* 32, no. 6, (2009), 455–475.
[90] Robert Axelrod, *Evolution of Cooperation* (New York: Basic Books, 1984).

augment state capabilities; and revolutionary states. The next subsections briefly discuss each, and then the section as a whole concludes with a unifying framework.

Negative Political Control, Comparative Advantage and Strategy

There are two approaches that may help to cast the crime-terror dynamic in a different light. Before looking at those, it is important to introduce the idea of negative political control. Terrorists benefit from the resources derived from criminality, but the benefits to criminals from collaboration with terrorists are less straightforward. Criminals may derive some profit from working with terrorists, but there are certainly other avenues of collaboration that they can pursue. What then, do criminals get out of their relationship with terrorists?

It is in the means of securing their objectives, rather than the objectives themselves, where criminals and terrorists are most likely to cooperate. Both groups use fear and intimidation. Terrorists use violence to persuade a population or a government to change policies. Criminals use violence to create space or metaphorical distance between their actions and the legal authorities. A criminal enterprise will be most successful when it can operate at some distance from law enforcement, and criminals use violence and fear to set the most favorable possible conditions for themselves. By distinguishing threats by the different ends they pursue, the convergence in means, like assassinations, vehicle IEDs and beheadings, appears less prominent. Both groups, however, use violence with the aim of making it difficult for others to govern effectively. This is one of the important goods, in an economic sense, that terrorists can offer criminals.

Along with the market for resources, there is a parallel market for governance, or better yet, a market for disrupting governance. As noted above, criminals often strive to create or find environments in which authorities have difficulty functioning, but criminals do not want to provide governance themselves. Patrick Radden Keefe used the phrase "jurisdictional arbitrage" to explain smugglers' propensity to find markets with space to operate.[91] Terrorists attack governing authorities with the aim of replacing a regime,

---

[91] Patrick Radden Keefe, *The Snakehead: An Epic Tale of the Chinatown Underworld and the American Dream* (New York: Doubleday, 2009)

and their tactics have the intermediate aim of disrupting governance. In that sense, both organizations seek to deny others the ability to govern. Criminals use the absence of governance to reduce the risk in pursuit of their profit, while terrorists want to deny others the ability to govern so they themselves may ultimately govern. While the ends are different, the intermediate step of denying governance is the same.

Both groups desire negative political control. That is to say, both groups desire to ensure that the legitimate authorities are relatively ineffective in certain spaces, without necessarily providing any of the services or public goods associated with government themselves. This is in contrast to positive political control, in which actors do provide these services. Terrorists may ultimately desire positive political control or to become the legitimate governing authority and provide services, but creating chaos, showing government incompetence and eroding confidence in government all fall into the category of negative political control. Much of the counterterrorism community has focused on the flow of resources between criminals and terrorists. The flow of governance, or the ability to achieve negative political control, may be just as important. The complete absence of governance, as discussed above, may not be attractive to either criminals or terrorists, but negative political control implies that illicit actors have the freedom to maneuver.

Terrorists may have the ultimate aim of governing, but one of the ways that terrorists can achieve this ultimate goal is by taking the intermediate step of denying others the ability to govern effectively. Criminals seek an identical intermediate step. They often have little interest in governing and providing things like security or social services, but they can benefit by denying others the ability to control or govern spaces effectively. This is most obvious in the physical world, but it can also apply to virtual spaces or financial sanctuaries. Criminals are capable of producing political or fear and terrorists are incapable of producing profit, but the two have different areas of operational expertise.

With this in mind, the first approach that may help elucidate the connectivity between criminals and terrorists is that of comparative advantage, first articulated by the political economist David Ricardo.[92] While often used in casual language on competition, comparative advantage theory was developed specifically to explain why countries benefit from trading goods. In short, Ricardo argued that countries benefit from trade because it allows them to specialize. The classic formulation dealt with the production and trade in cloth and wine between Britain and Portugal. If Britain were relatively more efficient at producing cloth and Portugal more efficient at producing wine, then the countries could consume more by specializing and trading. This is true even if one country is the most efficient at making all products, because the theory deals with relative efficiency.[93] In the case in which one country is better at everything, letting the less-efficient country focus on what it does best still makes everyone better off by increasing the aggregate output.

In the case of criminal and terrorist interaction, there are markets for resources and for political chaos. Generally speaking, criminals are better at producing resources, and terrorists excel at producing political chaos. While criminals might do more than dabble in political chaos and violence far exceeding normal levels seen in drug markets, as is the case in Mexico, a primary interest in crime seems to limit their political activity.[94] Likewise, terrorists might engage in criminal acts to support their operations, as al-Qa'ida in the Islamic Maghreb has done with such activities as kidnapping for ransom, but their ultimate end is political.[95] Given the primary interests of each group, which require a degree of specialization, the theory of comparative advantage suggests that the two should be engaged in a trade of goods and services.

A theory of illicit comparative advantage helps to articulate the convergence in crime and terror in a particular way, but it has its limitations. Comparative advantage is generally premised on the idea that more is better. More cloth and wine are better than less, and no one is really worse off if he or she obtains more of these goods. That may

---

[92] See David Ricardo's *On the Principles of Political Economy and Taxation*, first published in 1817.
[93] For a summary see Roy Ruffin, "David Ricardo's Discovery of Comparative Advantage," *History of Political Economy* 34, no. 4 (Winter 2002) 727–748.
[94] For a discussion, see George W. Grayson, *Mexico: Narco-Violence and a Failed State?* (New Brunswick: Transaction Publishers, 2011).
[95] Andrew Lebovich, "AQIM Returns in Force in Northern Algeria," *CTC Sentinel*, September 2001, available at www.ctc.usma.edu/posts/aqim-returns-in-force-in-northern-algeria.

not be true for the illicit marketplace. Criminals, while demanding some level of political instability, often abhor complete chaos.[96] It is hard to earn money and even harder to hold on to it in such environments. That is why individuals like Monzer al-Kassar often base their operations in developed countries. Criminals want enough space in which to operate, but they do not want an entire breakdown of government or civil society. Similarly, terrorists want resources, but an overaccumulation of them often erodes the ideological commitment of its members and turns the group into a criminal enterprise, much as happened with the FARC in Colombia.[97] In that sense, there may be output levels, for either criminality or terrorism, that become undesirable for partners.

Given this, there are limits to the comparative advantage paradigm. An alternative formulation of the problem could draw on game theory, and specifically noncooperative equilibrium.[98] In noncooperative game theory, actors often want to coordinate but it occurs only when the strategies to do so are self-enforcing. There is no contract or enforcement mechanism to ensure the groups work together beyond the benefit they get from pursuing a specific strategy. From this perspective, the criminal and the terrorist must independently determine how much of their effort they want to allocate to resource production and to negative political control. They must also decide whether they want to cooperate by sharing versus consuming their outputs, either economic profit or political turbulence. Any equilibrium outcome is likely to depend on the relative production capabilities of the groups and the relative demand for their individual products, which may well be driven by environmental or contextual factors.

For example, one could generate a game-theoretic problem whereby a group of terrorists want to achieve a maximal level of governmental instability and can produce a certain level of it based on their allocation of resources across the fields of terrorist operations and crime. Criminals want to maximize profits, and a certain level of challenge to their government probably improves their ability to generate those profits. Like the terrorists, the criminals can decide how much effort they want to expend

---

[96] For an example contradicting the link between failed states and global threats, see Stewart Patrick, "Weak states and global threats: Fact or fiction?," *Washington Quarterly* 29, no. 2 (2006) 27–53.

[97] Saab and Taylor, 2009.

[98] For more on noncooperative equilibrium, see James Morrow, *Game Theory for Political Scientists* (Princeton, NJ: Princeton University Press, 1994).

challenging the government versus pursuing criminal profits. Each group provides an intermediate good that the other group values, but interests of the two groups are not directly aligned. The two actors allocate their resources and decide how much to share with the other independent of each other.

With that general framework, it is possible to generate some predictions about cooperation that are counterintuitive. For example, terrorists and criminals might be less likely to cooperate in failed or poor states. At the "upper boundary" of political or institutional instability, terrorists may need fewer resources to sustain themselves and challenge the government, since there is little government to challenge. Similarly, criminals will require less political chaos in a failed or economically poor state, since they will already operate with a high degree of autonomy. A game-theoretic explanation would thereby seem to contradict conventional wisdom and suggest that there is little incentive for criminals and terrorists to cooperate in failed or poor states, since both parties can achieve their ends independently in such a situation.

Rather than failed or poor states promoting crime-terror interaction, more capable or developed states may in fact be those that generate connectivity and convergence. As an environment becomes more hostile to illicit actors (meaning that governance and law enforcement within it becomes more effective), specialization and trade may become more valuable to criminals and terrorists. If law enforcement can target and prosecute criminal elements successfully, while limiting terrorists' fund raising ability, then both criminal and terrorist elements are likely to benefit from cooperation with each other. In more developed countries, criminals' challenges to governance and terrorists' pursuit of criminal activity may be relatively inefficient—in other words, criminals' allocation of effort to produce negative political control and terrorists' allocation of effort to generate illicit profits may be a suboptimal strategy for each group. As a government's access to resources increases, each party is more likely to allocate effort toward its comparative advantage and then provide assistance to the other.

The predicted relationship between state resources and connectivity or convergence in the illicit marketplace differs from the resource scarcity argument after the political dimension is added. When negative political control becomes a good in itself that illicit actors want to consume, then the interrelationship between criminal and terrorist elements in the marketplace begins to look much different. This argument is referred to as the comparative advantage explanation of connectivity, drawn from the fact that actors have incentive to specialize on their relative strength and then to cooperate.

By unpacking the first assumption, the relationship among state capability, poverty and crime terror-interaction, there are at least two competing explanations: resource scarcity and comparative advantage. To this point, however, the exposition has continued to presume that governments and illicit actors are adversaries. This is not always the case, and it is equally important to consider how that might affect predications about the behavior of illicit actors in the global marketplace.

State Sponsorship and the Hidden Hand

The prior discussion examined causal arguments that explain illicit activity based on different governmental resource levels and assuming an adversarial relationship between the state and criminal actors. There are a similar set of arguments that link crime-terror connectivity among states that have a cooperative relationship with illicit actors.

One explanation draws on path dependence, or the idea that history matters. It is important to appreciate the possibility of common historical origins across both terrorist groups and organized crime enterprises. It is easy to think, particularly in the West, that terrorists and criminals always operate in opposition to state forces. This, however, is a simplistic representation of interests and institutional structures. Just as some states cultivate militant nonstate actors to pursue national or transnational security goals, they may also have an incentive to develop criminal enterprises for economic ends. Although the line between licit and illicit commercial dealings seems straightforward, it is historically opaque. The relationship among political elites, security services and organized criminals is deeply intertwined in much of the world.

State sponsored terrorism, or a country's use of violent substate groups in pursuit of its goals, has been an important tool of international statecraft throughout history. State-sponsored terrorism, some argue, reached its peak in the 1980s, with states like Libya,

Iran, Syria and Soviet Union leading the way.[99] The end of the Cold War, which meant a decline in support from the Soviet state, slowed the tide of state-sponsored attacks. Globalization also played a part in the decline of state-sponsored terrorism, and, according to this narrative, the benefits from state sponsored terrorism became offset by the increasing costs of being labeled a rogue regime. The only countries formally designated by the U.S. Department of State as state sponsors of terrorism are Cuba, Iran, Sudan and Syria, the last of which was so designated in 1993.[100] While many measures suggest that state sponsored terrorism is on the decline, the relationship among states, political parties and substate violence remains a ubiquitous aspect of national and international politics. Pakistan's support for LeT is a prime example of a state's support for a violent group, and citizens in Gulf States have also been historically identified as financial supporters of violent groups.[101]

There are a number of reasons why countries may choose to support terrorist groups. The terrorist group may offer a way of fighting a stronger opponent without a state engaging in a head-on confrontation. It may also provide the supporter with a measure of plausible deniability, while limiting a conflict's potential escalation.[102] A state's support of a terrorist group does come with a cost. Once a state cultivates a terrorist group, the individuals who run the group may disobey their state sponsors or carry out operations that are more violent than its sponsor intends. In that sense, there is a moral hazard involved with supporting terrorist groups, and this may well explain why many countries avoid the practice or engage in it sparingly.[103] A state's choice to support terrorist groups and accept the concordant risks may also serve as a bargaining signal to its adversaries. As such, it may increase the likelihood that any bargaining fails, but it

---

[99] Daniel Byman, "The Changing Nature of State Sponsorship of Terrorism," the Saban Center for Middle East Policy at The Brookings Institution, analysis paper no. 16, May 2008.

[100] See Department of State, "State Sponsors of Terrorism," available at www.state.gov/j/ct/list/c14151.htm.

[101] Maurice R. Greenberg, William F. Wechsler, Lee S. Woolsey *Terrorist Financing: Report of an Independent Task Force Sponsored by the Council on Foreign Relations* (New York: Council on Foreign Relations, 2002).

[102] Byman, 2005.

[103] Navin A. Bapat, "Understanding the State Sponsorship of Militant Groups," *British Journal of Political Science* 42, no. 1 (January 2012), 1–29.

could also help the sponsor achieve a favorable negotiated settlement.[104] The empirical assessment of this argument suggests that weak states and great powers can benefit from sponsoring terrorism. When states do sponsor terrorist entities, responsibility for managing the sponsorship usually falls to the intelligence or security services, as it does in Pakistan through the ISI and Iran through the Army of the Guardians of the Islamic Revolution (IRGC).

While there is a large literature on organized crime, the concept of state-sponsored criminal groups is underdeveloped among scholars. Criminals may infiltrate a government or corrupt a political system, turning a country into a client state. Political transitions or breakdowns in government may offer organized criminals the opportunity to expand, but they may also find success in stable and well-resourced political systems as well.[105] Although these examples capture the complex relationship between the state and criminal entities, they are not the same as state-sponsored criminal activity.

One example of this activity may be seen in North Korea's use of diplomatic privileges to smuggle an array of illicit goods around the globe.[106] In many cases, state sponsorship of organized crime may be more subtle. Prior to Russia's invasion of Georgia in 2008, there was a massive cyberattack targeting government and civilian systems. The Russian government claimed that it was not involved in the attack and that it was the work of political activists. By most accounts, the attacks were conducted by hackers connected to the organized crime world.[107] Countries also build criminal networks to subvert sanctions, which has proved to be a modestly successful strategy in the Balkans, Iran, North Korea and Pakistan. In short, governments may foster both terrorist and criminal enterprises. Much as a state's interaction with terrorist groups is managed at the clandestine level, a state's support of criminals is most often managed through its intelligence and security services.

---

[104] Ibid.

[105] For a discussion across cases, see Misha Glenny, 2008; Moises Naim, *Illicit: How Smugglers, Traffickers and Counterfeiters are Hijacking the Global Economy* (Doubleday: New York, 2005).

[106] Chestnut, 2007.

[107] John Markoff, "Before the Gunfire, Cyberattacks," *New York Times*, 12 August 2008, available at www.nytimes.com/2008/08/13/technology/13cyber.html?_r=0.

If one acknowledges that the relationship among states, their politicians, security services and organized criminal networks can be cooperative, then there is ample reason to expect connectivity between terrorist and criminal actors on behalf of the state as well. Ironically, the clandestine agents that orchestrate these connections may literally be the invisible men in the analysis here, as governments are often better than illicit actors at hiding their operatives. This may account for at least some of the suspicious individuals identified in the network analysis discussed previously. In this sense, the two-player interaction, or game, that was developed in the prior section may have a third player that acts as an arbiter or intermediary. Countries that either foster or maintain illicit marketplaces in their perceived national interests may play an important role in facilitating connectivity among criminals and terrorists. Such state-sponsored marketplaces may also prove relevant in explaining the prominence of transnational relationships, as many countries seek benefits from cross-border connections in areas like subverting sanctions, transferring arms or strengthening positions against international adversaries.

A country is likely to utilize substate actors like terrorist groups or criminal enterprises to augment its capabilities when it has relatively few resources. Here, the government's incentive for cultivating criminals and terrorists is likely different from the adversarial relationship. Resource-poor states prone to conflicts have an interest in criminal activity to generate additional funds. Terrorists, meanwhile, offer the government a cost-effective method of menacing its adversary. Both are attractive to resource-constrained governments.

Revolutionary States

This section has thus far distinguished potential explanations for the connectivity between terrorists and criminals along two dimensions. The first is resources and the second is the propensity of a state to sponsor illicit activities. While the comparative advantage explanation focuses on well-resourced governments that have an adversarial relationship with illicit actors, one also must consider the cases of well-resourced countries that cooperate with illicit elements. These instances represent the classic revolutionary state.

Resource-rich countries that fund illicit substate activities usually do so for revolutionary purposes, much as the Soviet Union did to spread communism during the Cold War. The Soviet Union used an array of irregular tactics, from fomenting riots in Eastern Europe to funding proxy military or paramilitary forces in Africa, Asia and South America. The revolutionary vanguard, in these instances, views itself as the protector and engine of revolutionary activity. While the classic notion of the revolutionary vanguard, in Marxism, holds that it is composed of part of the proletariat and is an engine operating among the working class, in many cases its members are part of an elite such as the Communist International.

Today, one can point to Iran as a relatively competent and well-resourced government that nonetheless chooses to export terrorism and criminality around the globe. The reach of the IRGC spans the world, as does Iran's clandestine financial network. The country continues to financially support activity in the Middle East, and it has historically backed attacks in places such as Europe and South America. The revolutionary state is willing to put its substantial resource base to work leveraging the available means of state power, including terrorist and criminal activity, in pursuit of internationalist and ideological aims. These states are often viewed in international politics as anti–status quo or rogue regimes.

Summarizing the Four Explanations

There are four possible competing explanations for crime-terror connectivity: resource scarcity, comparative advantage, augmenting state capabilities and revolutionary states. This is presented in Figure 10, which incorporates states' resource levels and their interest in sponsorship. Each of the four explanations for crime-terror connectivity is plausible, even if some seem less likely. Connectivity may be driven by resource constraints in states with an adversarial policy, as in the resource scarcity argument; by resource abundance in an adversarial state in the comparative advantage model; by resource constraints in a state sponsoring illicit activity in the augmented capability theory; or by resource-rich sponsoring states, per the revolutionary argument.

Figure 10: Competing Causal Models of Crime-Terror Connectivity

		Adversarial	Cooperative
State Resources	High	Comparative Advantage (i.e. Mexico)	Revolutionary State (i.e. Iran)
	Low	Resource Competition (i.e. Somalia)	Augment State Capabilities (i.e. Pakistan)

State Sponsorship

Rather than simply stop at a proposal of four possible explanations, this paper continues in the next section to test the competing theories to gain a more complete understanding of crime-terror connectivity. The empirical results in the next section will help identify the arguments with the best empirical support.

Hubs of Connectivity in the Illicit Marketplace

The nature of the empirical data utilized to examine the network structure of illicit activity also offers a first or unique look into the potential drivers of crime-terror connectivity. There is a long history of using national factors such as political, economic and demographic variables to explain the variance in conflict, civil war or terrorism across countries.[108] Because the social network developed for this project includes the known areas of operation for each individual, the data can be structured to capture characteristics such as the concentration of illicit actors, the connectivity between criminals and terrorists and the prominence of transnational linkages. That data allow us to examine the four explanations and assess the competing theories of crime-terror connectivity.

---

[108] Alan B. Krueger and Jitka Maleckova, "Education, Poverty and Terrorism: Is There a Causal Connection?," *Journal of Economic Perspectives* 17, no. 4 (November 2003), 119–144; Alberto Abadie, "Poverty, Political Freedom, and the Roots of Terrorism" *American Economic Review* 96, no. 2 (Spring 2006), 50–56; James A. Piazza, "Rooted in Poverty?: Terrorism, Poor Economic Development, and Social Cleavages," *Terrorism and Political Violence* 18, no. 1 (Spring 2006), 159–177; S. Brock Blomberg, Gregory D. Hessa and Akila Weerapana, "Economic Conditions and Terrorism," *European Journal of Political Economy* 20, no. 2 (Spring 2004), 463–478; Quan Li and Drew Schaub, "Economic Globalization and Transnational Terrorism: A Pooled Time Series Analysis," *Journal of Conflict Resolution* 48, no. 2 (April 2004), 230–259; Quan Li, "Does Democracy Promote or Reduce Transnational Terrorist Incidents?" *Journal of Conflict Resolution* 49, no. 2 (March 2005), 278–297; Patrick Regan, "Conditions of Successful Third Party Intervention in Intrastate Conflicts," *Journal of Conflict Resolution* 40, no. 4 (July 1996), 336–359. Michael Doyle and Nicholas Sambanis, "International Peacebuilding: A Theoretical and Quantitative Analysis," *American Political Science Review* 94, no. 4 (Fall 2000), 779–801; Dylan Balch-Lindsay and Andrew Enterline, "Killing Time: The World Politics of Civil War Duration, 1820–1992," *International Studies Quarterly* 44, no. 4 (Fall 2000), 615–642; James D. Fearon, "Why Do Some Civil Wars Last So Much Longer Than Others?" *Journal of Peace Research* 41, no. 3 (Summer 2004), 275–301; Monica Duffy Toft, *Securing the Peace: The Durable Settlement of Civil Wars* (Princeton: Princeton University Press, 2009); James Fearon and David Laitin, "Ethnicity, Insurgency, and Civil War," *American Political Science Review* 97, no. 1 (Winter 2003), 75–90; Paul Collier and Anke Hoeffler, "Greed and Grievance in Civil War," *Oxford Economic Papers* 56, no. 4 (2004), 563–595; Havard Hegre, "Toward a Democratic Civil Peace? Democracy, Political Change, and Civil War, 1816–1992," *American Political Science Review* 95, no. 1 (Winter 2001), 33–48; Karl R. DeRouen and David Sobek, "The Dynamics of Civil War Duration and Outcome," *Journal of Peace Research* 41, no. 3 (Summer 2003), 303–320.

The empirical analysis involved two steps. The first focused on restructuring the data. The social network data captured interpersonal connections and the areas of each individual's operations. This data was restructured to reflect the number of illicit actors in each country, which is a measure of total concentration.[109] This data could be further parsed to show whether the people in the network were coded as terrorists, narcotics smugglers, organized criminals or the like. Since the social network data reflected instances in which terrorists and other criminals knew one another, those could similarly be summed at the country level to generate a measure of crime-terror connectivity. One final measure, transnational connectivity, was developed by looking at instances in which individuals were linked to people in other countries. The drivers of connections across countries may well be distinct from the concentration of connections within a country. For example, the leaders of the Sinaloa crime syndicate in Mexico will have a web of connections in that country to support their local operations, but some will have cross-border connections to facilitate transport, sales and finance.

This section summarizes the results across these different ways of counting or characterizing the social connections of illicit actors at the national level. Each of the variables exists as a count of individuals or relationships, for example, the total number of illicit actors or illicit relationships summed for each country. The same method was used to capture crime-terror connectivity and transnational ties.[110]

The statistical tests rely on a series of variables common in cross-sectional political and economic studies. The economic variables in the study are GDP (logged) and GDP growth rates. The GDP number captures the aggregate resource level within a country, which is an important part of the theoretical explanations discussed previously. The other key variable is the countries' relationships with the illicit actors: adversarial or cooperative. While it is difficult to observe a country's use of substate actors, it is possible to look at a country's propensity to engage in interstate disputes. Countries

---

[109] The analysis weights all areas of operation equally and therefore does not distinguish individuals who concentrate their time in one location relative to other areas of their operation.

[110] As a result, the empirical analysis used statistical models appropriate for count data, which is different from typical linear regression. The linear regression model assumes that the dependent variable, or the factor to be explained, follows a normal bell curve distribution. Count variables rarely exhibit such a distribution, meaning other analytic models, like a negative binomial, are better suited for this data.

that engage in external disputes with greater frequency, particularly countries with relatively low levels of resources, should have a greater incentive to augment their resource levels than other countries. The militarized interstate dispute data show how conflict-prone a country is, and therefore whether it has an incentive to support substate actors to enhance its security.[111] The analysis then interacts the GDP and the dispute variables to examine whether illicit activity is similar in resource-rich and resource-poor countries prone to disputes. The analysis also includes a variable that reflects the countries' failed status, drawn from the Failed State Index maintained by a U.S. nonprofit group called the Fund for Peace.[112] The remaining variables control for political and demographic factors like autocracy-democracy levels (polity score), population and density and Internet use.

Perhaps the most dominant narrative explaining connections among illicit actors links illicit activity to state failure and poverty, which is termed the resource scarcity model. The state failure explanation is empirically supported, while the poverty argument is not. State failure is associated with a greater concentration of illicit actors within a country. The complementary explanation that poverty generates more illicit actors does not get support from the data here. In fact, the opposite is true. The countries with the most illicit actors present within them are those with the largest economies as measured by the log of GDP. Both measures' finding on the size of an economy suggests that illicit actors may be driven more by the opportunity of lucrative, developed markets than a reaction to resource scarcity. The analysis also shows that the level of democracy (autocracy-democracy score) proved meaningful, with the most illicit actors found in countries with high democracy scores. For example, both the United States (high GDP) and Somalia (state failure) have high concentrations of illicit actors. This seems to come from the fact that conditions fostering illicit activities exist on both ends of the spectrum, even if the drivers at each end are different. The remaining demographic variables like population size did not prove to be significant predictors of individual concentration within a country.

---

[111] The analysis here includes all MIDs, recognizing that disputes can be characterized by different levels of intensity.

[112] The website can be accessed at http://ffp.statesindex.org/.

The relative effect of these variables is found in Figure 11, which shows that the variables do not necessarily have equal predictive power. The variable that seems to exert the strongest correlation is economy size measured by log GDP, followed by the failed state score. A marginal increase of log GDP in the midrange from $72.5 billion to $197 billion increases the total number of illicit actors by 110 percent. The Failed State Index also shows significant correlation, with a 20 point increase in the midrange from 80 to 100 more than doubling the predicted number of individuals, from 20 to 47. The final variable that correlates with the total number of individuals is polity, but the graphic shows that the effect is reasonably small. Moving from the most autocratic country (-10) to the most democratic (10) only produced an 8-person increase, from 5 to 17, and such a move is extreme and unlikely.[113]

Figure 11: Aggregate Individuals

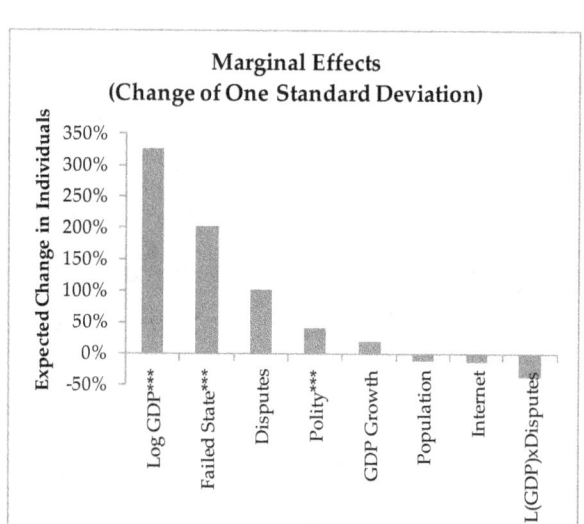

Note: Statistical significance denoted in p-values *<0.1, **<0.05, and ***<0.01.

The drivers of connectivity, specifically crime-terror connectivity, bear some similarities and differences to the aggregate count. Crime-terror connectivity examines the total number of relationships that cross between terrorists and criminal actors in each country, controlling for the total number of links per country. Despite the fact that the

_____

[113] Subsets of the data can be used to examine whether factors that correlated with terrorist activity also correlated with criminal activity. It is interesting to note that wealthier countries tended to have higher numbers of criminals and terrorists, whereas failed state status generally correlated with terrorism.

connectivity of criminal and terrorist actors is something distinct from the aggregate illicit activity, national-level cross-section explanations reference similar factors such as state failure and poor economies.

Figure 12: Crime-Terror Connectivity

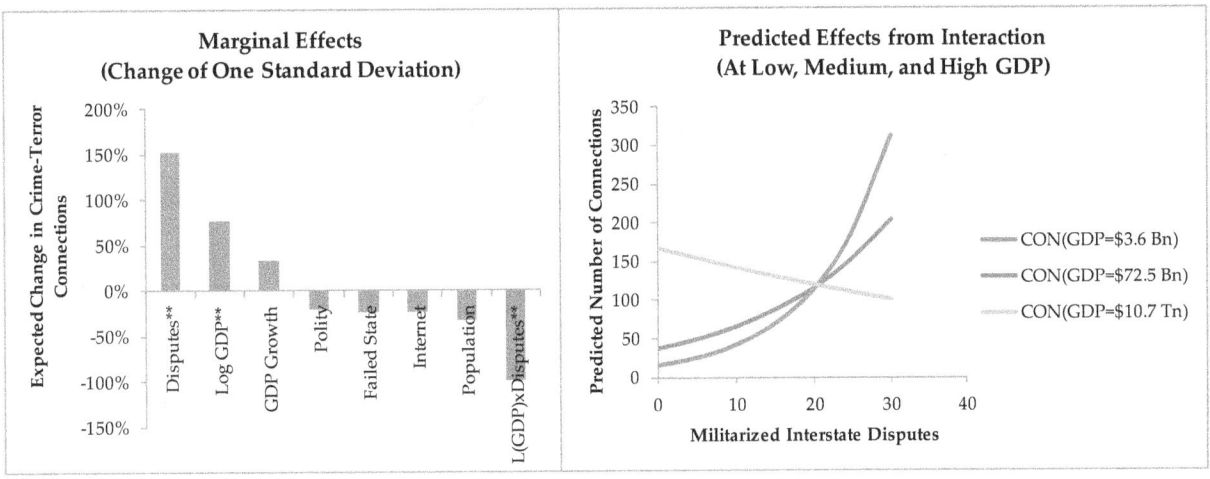

Note: Statistical significance denoted in p-values *<0.1, **<0.05, and ***<0.01.

Much as the informal comparative advantage model predicted, failing or failed state status is not statistically associated with crime-terror connectivity. This suggests that the conventional wisdom is misplaced and that the drivers behind aggregate illicit activity and crime-terror convergence might be different. While the failed state measure does not have a meaningful explanatory effect on connectivity, GDP does positively correlate. Instead of connecting in environments in which states are relatively impotent, terrorists and criminals are more likely to converge in richer states that are likely to have more resource capacity as predicted by the model. The number of disputes also correlates with the count of illicit actors, and it is the strongest predictive variable in the connectivity analysis. There is a caveat tied to militarized disputes and the interaction effect with GDP. When the GDP and dispute counts are interacted, there is an inverse statistically significant relationship. These types of interactions are often best assessed graphically, which may be found in the right pane of Figure 12. In short, the number of illicit actors increases as both GDP and disputes increase, but this effect reverses itself in states with higher GDP. In other words, the number of illicit actors increases as disputes increase in poorer countries, but that relationship reverses in countries with high resource levels. The analysis shows that crime-terror connectivity is generally prevalent

75

in two environments: The first is resource-rich countries and the second is resource poor-countries that are prone to conflict. The predicted relationships are shown in Figure 12.

The graphs in Figure 12 again illustrate that economics and a state's incentives play a significant role in crime-terror connectivity. Doubling the median GDP of $72.5 billion to $197 billion increases the predicted number of crime-terror relationships from 57 to 77. The other variables that correlate with connectivity are the disputes and the interaction term. The right side of Figure 12 shows the relationship between dispute initiation and crime-terror connectivity at different levels of GDP. This analysis provides empirical validation for two of the four explanations: comparative advantage and augmenting state capabilities. There is little to support the conventional wisdom associated with the resource scarcity theory or the concept of revolutionary states. Figure 13 shows the explanations that get the most support in green.

Figure 13: Explanation and Empirical Support

		Comparative Advantage (i.e. Mexico)	Revolutionary State (i.e. Iran)
State Resources	High		
	Low	Resource Competition (i.e. Somalia)	Augment State Capabilities (i.e. Pakistan)
		Adversarial	Cooperative

State Sponsorship

Note: Shaded regions have empirical support. Unshaded regions have weak or no empirical support.

To move from beyond the statistical realm into concrete examples, Table 5 shows the countries that have the most individuals and the most convergence between criminal and terrorist actors as represented by social connections. Countries with the most illicit actors tied to this network include Mexico and Colombia, owing in large part to their illegal narcotics businesses and terrorist groups. The United States, as the world's largest consumer economy and a frequent target of illicit goods, also ranks high. It is followed by countries such as India and Pakistan with well-documented underworld economies that blend profit motives with ideological drive. There are also a number of countries that play an important role, often unwittingly, in facilitating illicit activity by providing sanctuary or access to the global financial system.

Table 5: Prominent Countries

Rank	Number of Individuals	Rank	Crime-Terror Convergence (by Link Count)
1	Mexico	1	Colombia
2	Colombia	2	United Arab Emirates
3	United States	3	India
4	India	4	United States
5	Pakistan	5	Russian Federation
6	United Arab Emirates	6	Pakistan
7	Afghanistan	7	South Africa
8	Syrian Arab Republic	8	Liberia
9	Spain	9	Belgium
10	Argentina	10	Mexico
11	Korea, Rep.	11	Thailand
12	Brazil	12	Tajikistan
13	Iraq	13	Syrian Arab Republic
14	Saudi Arabia	14	Spain
15	Nicaragua	15	Panama

The list of the countries with the most illicit actors, as the analysis above shows, is not quite the same as the list of countries with the greatest connectivity among criminals and terrorists. It is also interesting to note that the list of countries with high crime-terror connectivity does not align with conventional wisdom, as it continues to challenge the resource scarcity argument. Eleven of the top fifteen countries on the convergence list are among the largest thirty economies in the world. Approximately 70 percent of the countries in which convergence is prominent are among the richest in the world. Only four, Liberia (4 disputes), Pakistan (17 disputes), Panama (8 disputes) and Tajikistan (5 disputes) are examples of small or resource-poor economies.

It seems as though convergence is most prominent in relatively wealthy countries, which by extension tend to have reasonably well-functioning governments. This may in fact help explain why convergence is more prominent in wealthy countries. Terrorist and criminal elements are only successful for extended periods of time when a state supports their efforts or when they can achieve negative political control—that is, deny others the ability to govern a certain space. That space may vary to include physical or legal spheres such as land or banking regulations. Groups may not need to work together in failed states, but the government may be a hidden hand. By contrast, denying governance in rich countries with capable government apparatuses is likely to prove far more difficult than in failed sates, making potential collaborations across illicit elements more valuable to terrorists and criminals.

The presence of transnational linkages is also distinct from aggregate activity or crime-terror connectivity. Transnational linkages make it more difficult to attack illicit networks, since they involve cooperation across jurisdictions. These connections also help to make the network more robust, since they are critical in moving people, resources and ideas into new markets given new opportunities. While crime-terror connectivity is driven in part by state capability and resources, the driver of transnational connections is slightly more complicated. In general, illicit actors generally want access to both underdeveloped and developed markets. The former allows a degree of sanctuary in which to pursue their activities, whereas the latter offer lucrative opportunities to sell illicit goods and to reinvest the ill-gotten gains.

It would stand to reason, then, that there is a nonlinear relationship between transnational connections and wealth. Illicit actors in relatively poor countries should be interested in maintaining ties with wealthier countries to gain access to their resource pools and the financial systems. Likewise, illicit actors in richer countries are likely to maintain connections with those in less-developed countries to leverage space with minimal law enforcement. The statistical analysis here does show that there is a nonlinear relationship between wealth and transnational connections. Contrary to the idea that connections are more prominent in impoverished states, the analysis shows that illicit actors want access to wealthy countries. Failed state status and the political regime are not meaningful correlates, but total population size negatively correlates with transnational connections. This is rather intuitive, since actors in smaller countries are more likely to link with those in larger markets.

The analysis above provides an interesting assessment of global illicit activity. It certainly has limitations, as with any type of study delving into the clandestine. This analysis is static and therefore captures relationships that have been documented over time. Some scholars have correctly identified that groups or individuals may work together for certain periods of time and then terminate their relations.[114] This is true, and ideally a dynamic network would account for this. At the same time, the analysis here suggests that convergence between those involved in different activities across the illicit universe is not exceptional. It is a regular course of doing business for many.

---

[114] Shelley and Picarelli, 2002.

CONCLUSIONS AND IMPLICATIONS

There are a number of important conclusions to be derived from this study. The first substantive conclusion deals with the level of connectivity across the network. Rather than finding multiple parallel or disconnected networks separated by geography and illicit activity, almost all of the 2,700-person sample is subsumed in a single large global structure. This should not be construed to say that the network is a cohesive organizational entity with a singular leadership or standard operating procedures. The phenomenon observed and documented here is a self-organizing complex system built through social connections from the bottom up that manifests in a global reach.

The network analysis also reveals some interesting characteristics about so-called kingpins. While there are people clearly atop the global illicit market, in terms of wealth, operational control and network connectivity, there are redundancies in the network structure. The redundancy in the network comes from a disproportionately high number of network ties among mid-level individuals. While these individuals are not empowered to the extent of the kingpins, removing the kingpins will not crash the network.[115] The redundancies found in the network help such a dark network reconstitute its activities quickly in the aftermath of the loss of a leader. There is often a period of uncertainty, fracturing and consolidation as less-connected or -empowered individuals vie for leadership, but history suggests that this process plays out relatively quickly.

The relative concentration of actors involved in different activities is instructive. The study began with a list of forty individuals involved in the illicit narcotics, arms and human smuggling businesses. Despite the initial emphasis on the criminal side of the illicit market, there are almost as many terrorists as narcotics traffickers in the final sample. This snapshot suggests at least some reasonable level of integration between the criminal and terrorist elements operating globally. Undoubtedly, there are some criminals who would knowingly refuse to work with terrorists, and there may be terrorists whose ideological convictions prevent them from working with criminals.

---

[115] Kenney, 2007 makes a similar argument.

Moral or ethical obstacles may impede cooperation for some, but this study suggests that many in the illicit network are not constrained in such a fashion.

The concentration also revealed another interesting and unexpected characteristic: the massive number of suspicious individuals. Almost half of those in the network were not directly identified as criminals or terrorists, but were suspected for involvement in illicit activities. The prominence of these actors may reflect the importance of operating across the licit and the illicit spheres. Since these people are not blacklisted or under indictments, they represent an opportunity for illicit actors to move funds into the licit financial system, to own licit businesses and to promote an air of legitimacy in their business dealings. Many of the individuals in the network would prefer to be seen as successful businesspeople in the licit space, and their "suspicious" connections can help them advance that agenda.

Not only does the analysis show a concentration of terrorists in the network, it also suggests that they are both well-connected and centrally located in the network. The terrorists are not banished to the margins or shunned by their criminal counterparts. Rather, they are almost as connected as the narcotics smugglers are, and also playing an important role in connecting disparate groups. An analysis of social connections shows that 35 percent of the links that criminals and suspicious individuals maintain cross into terrorism.

Although the prominence of connectivity is clear in this effort, it begs the question why this insight has eluded the policy community deeply involved in addressing the issue. One reason lies in the distinction between means and ends. The policy community, and by extension the analytical community, have generally distinguished among illicit actors according to their ends. The economic ends of illegal narcotics dealers and organized criminals are different from the political ends of the terrorists. At times, the violence associated with crime has driven governments to pursue groups like the Mafia and the Cali Cartel, but it is often treated as a law enforcement issue. Terrorists, with their political ends, may be a nuisance or may present a significant threat depending on their ideology and capabilities. The distinction according to ends may have masked a convergence in means that is increasingly prominent.

Both criminals and terrorists pursue resources and sanctuary, albeit in different amounts. Criminals pursue profit and terrorists require resources, but that is not their only area of overlap. Terrorists wish to present a political challenge in the hopes of exercising control over territory, and criminals look for different types of sanctuary in which to operate insulated from law enforcement. Both groups seek to achieve negative political control by denying legal authorities the ability to govern a space. The end goals of criminals and terrorists differ, but they both require political space and resources in the intermediate stage.

Aggregate illicit activity, measured by the number of network members by country, suggests that failed states do attract or promote illicit activity. At the same time, aggregate activity was found to be more prominent in richer countries, which challenges the idea that illicit activity is driven by poverty. The link between economics and criminality is complicated, with divergent expectations based on an assessment of conditions that drive push and pull. There may be fewer legitimate means to amass wealth in poor countries, pushing individuals toward crime, but the ample opportunities that exist in wealthy countries may pull people toward criminality.

There is little evidence to support the idea that crime-terror connectivity is driven by poverty or resource scarcity. In addition, there is no evidence that state failure promotes connectivity. Although it may be easier or safer for criminals and terrorists to cooperate in those environments, convenience is not a particularly strong causal explanation for this, and it gets no empirical support here. Crime-terror connectivity is best explained by economic conditions, state incentives to sponsor substate groups and the interaction effect observed between these two factors. Generally speaking, the most connectivity is seen in resource-rich countries that have little incentive to support substate actors (comparative advantage theory) and resource-poor countries that are incentivized to support criminal or terrorist groups (augment state capabilities theory).

Methodologically, this analysis shows how data science and big data can shed light on a pressing issue, one that is usually viewed as opaque. Gathering, exploiting and structuring data, in this case open-source data, can offer a unique way of approaching a problem. This also shows how multifaceted data can be. Different data structures and analytics, applied to the same underlying data, can be used to assess different questions and reach different conclusions.

Implications

The implications for the study are far-reaching and present some difficult challenges ahead. There is a tendency in the policy community to see the dangers of crime-terror connectivity as stemming from poor countries and failed states, but this only speaks to part of the problem. Although aggregate activity correlates with failed states, connectivity and aggregate activity is tied to wealthy countries. U.S. and global strategy aimed at addressing crime-terror issues should reflect that connectivity is a distributed issue and not constrained to any one type of state. The data analysis here shows that 122 countries are connected by more than 1,000 transnational relationships, so strategy and tactics need to address both wealthy countries and poor countries that have incentives for supporting this behavior.

The emphasis on failed states by national security and law enforcement authorities is in part driven by an illusion; namely, if the weak or nonexistent governments in failed states can be replaced with functional institutions, then the threat from criminal and terror groups will decline. This might be a red herring. The reality, as the United States has learned over repeated campaigns, is that building institutions or solving the problem of failed states is anything but simple, and it does not seem to be the linchpin in combating the illicit global threat network. If criminal and terror connectivity is a characteristic of failed states as opposed to functioning states, then it can be alleviated by building a functioning government in such states. But, if connectivity is a characteristic of wealthy and functioning states, then building a functioning government in failed states does not necessarily solve the problem. The solution becomes more complicated.

The analysis shows that wealthy, developed countries are prone to dense crime-terror connectivity, and there are reasons that such countries might attract illicit activity despite the presence of a functioning government and law enforcement agencies. The allure of accessing wealthy markets and individuals may be too much for criminals or terrorists to pass up. These markets offer criminals and terrorists the opportunity to make illicit profits, reinvest assets, gain know-how, access material resources and choose among an array of targets. The challenge of combating crime and terror connectivity in such markets lies at the intersection between licit and illicit activity. The illicit economy is estimated to be as large as 20 to 30 percent of the global economy, or

$50 to $70 trillion. That money is not put under mattresses or tucked away in warehouses. Ill-gotten gains make their way into banks, investment vehicles, real estate and other investment opportunities. Al-Qa'ida, for example, once tried its luck with a stock account in Chicago.[116]

Wealthy economies are lucrative avenues for illicit actors looking to profit or find symbolic targets, even those conventionally believed to live in the shadows. The challenge for a government in these environments is less about improving law enforcement than it is recognizing the link between the licit and illicit financial spheres. The reason that the network portrayed in this study is so heavily populated with suspicious individuals is that illicit actors seek ways to access the legitimate market, and suspicious individuals provide a cutout or an indirect connection to it.

Attacking the crime-terror network solely by targeting illicit activity is a half measure in developed countries. The line between the licit and illicit can be obscure. Mexican drug organizations that have had difficulty moving money out of the United States for example, have found success investing in small towns along the U.S.-Mexico border, creating a boom in local economies. U.S. authorities will go after money linked to illicit activity, but once it is introduced into the local economy, distinguishing between the licit and illicit funds becomes difficult. This is further complicated by the complex financial transactions that have become commonplace among the more sophisticated individuals in the illicit world. The authorities tasked with addressing this issue seem to be losing the financial arms race as the adversaries' financiers often manage to stay a step ahead.

The first challenge confronting law enforcement and national security authorities is that there is a skill gap. While there are many qualified and motivated people in the U.S. government, much of the community has an enemy-centric approach to business and financial intelligence. Once heightened-risk individuals involved in business or finance are identified, the government might look at their call history, personal interactions and sympathies. The intelligence process is much like building a file on a criminal subject.

---

[116] Annie Sweeney, "Al-Qaida Operative Invested with Chicago Brokerage House in 2005," *Chicago Tribune*, 21 June 2011, available at http://articles.chicagotribune.com/2011-06-21/business/ct-met-terrorism-financing-20110621_1_al-qaida-qaida-al-ghamdi.

While their business interests may be listed, detailed financial due diligence or forensic accounting is often missing. Looking at call history to see whether an individual has connections to illicit actors is only a start. Identifying financial irregularities is critical to tracking dirty money, questionable transactions and illicit actors.

At present, many government agencies are not training analysts in the intelligence or defense communities to think in this way or to conduct such analyses. It does happen, but it remains an exception. The law enforcement community, like the DEA, which has a longer history in tracking the destination of ill-gotten gains, is better equipped to conduct such analysis. Many agencies have recruited accountants for exactly that reason. That said, because financial markets evolve at such a rapid pace, it is difficult for such agencies to keep up. Developed countries will remain attractive destinations for criminals and terrorists until this can be addressed.

Authorizations will also play a critical role in attacking the global network of terror and crime. The Department of Defense assigns resources to such programs as counterterrorism, counternarcotics and counterproliferation discretely. These are lines drawn according to authorizations. Counternarcotics resources in South Asia or Latin America are not authorized for use in counterterrorism. Occasionally, clear connectivity allows for dual use, which is to say that joint resources can be applied, but often resources are tasked to a specific functional area. The ubiquitous nature of crime-terror connectivity suggests that maintaining such rigid boundaries may not always be the most effective approach, and utilizing resources and techniques associated with counterterrorism in conjunction with counternarcotics may yield the best results.

That said, this project should not necessarily be interpreted as a call for new authorizations. It could be argued that the current set of authorizations rely on distinctions between crime and terror that are increasingly out of touch with operational realities, and the connectivity identified in this project might support such a position. Many of the dedicated professionals that confront these challenges on a daily basis, however, suggest that the current set of authorizations is adequate. Instead, actors across the interagency national security apparatus must understand the authorizations granted to partner organizations, in order to design more comprehensive strategies for tackling these interconnected challenges. There appears to be no easy and straightforward answer, but the debate itself will be important in either redefining authorizations or using the current ones more effectively.

Perhaps the greatest impediment to crippling the global illicit network is political will. Many governments, including that of the United States, work to impede activities in the global illicit marketplace, but the political will to pursue this course goes only so far. Policy makers recognize that crime has always been a feature of modern society and is not going away. Some level of it, therefore, must be tolerated. The question then becomes when crime or its derivative effects, such as providing material support for terrorists, rises to a level that is intolerable. That red line creates an opaque boundary separating the acceptable from the unacceptable crime. The licit side represents its own challenge. There are tools aimed at preventing illicit funds from flowing into the licit system, but they cannot keep pace given the sheer volume of financial transactions. The system is set up to identify or block the worst offenders, but the political will to go beyond those cases is absent in the United States. The problem of illicit funds entering the licit marketplace is further complicated by the fact that any serious solutions will have a transnational component, given the reach of the global criminal and terrorist network. It is not just a matter of political will within the United States but globally.

The network analyzed here focuses, in part, on physical location and geography, but illicit activity is increasingly virtual. The same people who are major players in the illegal narcotics, arms and organized crime spaces will also move into the virtual space given the right opportunity, just as any savvy entrepreneur would. Criminals already use the virtual space for communications and counterintelligence. Many of the leading organized crime syndicates, such as the Russians, have been investing in cyber capabilities. The growth of cyberspace and cybercrime will present another challenge while empowering illicit actors. Interestingly enough, the greatest threats in the cyber arena will likely come from developed countries or states that sponsor malevolent cyber activity, much similar to the existing network described here.

Rather than the interconnection between criminals and terrorists receding, it will likely continue to increase. If so, the traditional distinctions between criminal and terrorist activity may prove a hindrance to policies addressing the evolving threat to global law and order. One of the most important steps in addressing this challenge will be the better use of information. As the available cache of information inevitably grows larger, leveraging and interrogating data in creative ways will play a critical role in identifying illicit activity and stopping the most dangerous offenders.

Appendix A

Table 6: Sample List of Forty Smugglers

Individual	Activity
An Soon Kim	Humans
Arkadi Gaydamak	Arms
Chaudhary Ehsan	Humans
Daniel Rendón Herrera	Narcotics
Haji Bashir Noorzai	Narcotics
Jean Bernaud Lasnaud	Arms
Leonid Minin	Arms
Marcos Arturo Beltran Levya	Narcotics
Rafael Caro-Quintero	Narcotics
Vicente Carrillo-Fuentes	Narcotics

www.ingramcontent.com/pod-product-compliance
Lightning Source LLC
Chambersburg PA
CBHW080321290526
45790CB00005B/2133